In Defense of Marriage

In Defense of Marriage

Joanna Magda Polenz, M.D.

Gardner Press, Inc.
New York

Although this book is based on my clinical experience and drawn from my many years of practice, all names and other personal data have been changed to preserve anonymity. If any person thinks he or she recognizes himself or herself in the clinical illustrations, it is only proof that we humans resemble one another and share some common problems.

Gardner Press, Inc.
19 Union Square West
New York 10003

Library of Congress Cataloging in Publication Data

Polenz, Joanna Magda, 1936-
In defense of marriage.

Bibliography: p.
Includes index.
1. Marriage. I. Title.
HQ728.P58 306.8 80-14163
ISBN 0-89876-013-5

Printed in the United States of America

To Daryl

Contents

Preface *ix*

1 **WHAT MARRIAGE IS AND ISN'T** *13*

What Marriage Offers

Criticisms of Marriage

The Strengths of Marriage

2 **STRESS ON MARRIAGE** *23*

Unresolved Early Stress

Unconscious Needs

Dealing With Stress

3 **SEX AND MARRIAGE** *37*

The Sexual Advantages of Marriage

Possible Sexual Problems

Separation

Differences in Appetite

Avoidance and Affairs

Obsessive Sex

Varieties of Marital Sex

Sexual Preference

The Advantages of Marital Sex

Changes

Foreplay

Variations

Oral Sex

Anal Sex

Alcohol and Marriage

Drugs

Pornography

Sadomasochism

Illness

Sex Manuals

4 **CHILDREN IN MARRIAGE** *89*

Contraception

Marriage and Children

Why and When To Have Children
Implications of Family Size
Implications of Boys or Girls
Family Life Without Children
Handicapped Children

5 **THE PRACTICAL SIDE OF MARRIAGE** *117*
Work
Male and Female Roles in Marriage
Money
Work and Money
Spending Money
Money as a Weapon
The Home
Possessions

6 **THE TENDER SIDE OF MARRIAGE** *145*
Love and Marriage
Companionship in Marriage
Recreation in Marriage
Support in Adversity

7 **PARTNERS IN MARRIAGE** *161*
Am I Right For Marriage?
Capacity for Intimacy
Tolerance for Frustration
Oversensitivity
Egocentricity
Physical Aspects
Maturity
Who Would Be Right For Me?
Unconscious Elements in Selecting a Spouse
Conscious Elements in Selecting a Spouse
Premarital Sex

8 **IN DEFENSE OF MARRIAGE** *187*

REFERENCES *191*

INDEX *197*

Preface

I reached the point of view expressed in this book in the course of my clinical work as a psychiatrist. For many years I have observed and treated people unable to cope with the problems of building a gratifying life for themselves. Most of them tend to turn to what they think will be easy solutions that lie outside themselves. By doing so they hope to avoid the inner confrontations that lead to change, which is always difficult and often painful. It seems easier to them to change their social environment than themselves. And though it is true that it is often easier to change social environments, such change often does not help. Unfortunately, building a life in this difficult world usually requires self-knowledge, discipline, an ability to handle diverse relationships with other people, self-confrontation, however unpleasant, and internal change.

I am concerned that many people today try to take this easier path in the central area of life—that is, in close human relationships in general and sexuality in particular. Recently it has become easier and more respectable to try alternate life styles in which people have sexual relations with more than just one special person—for example, so-called group marriages. Proponents of alternate life styles suggest that changing these external arrangements lets people bypass many problems of relationships. In fact, these alternate life styles do not do that; nor do they in any other way improve the lot of the people who try them. Rather, they compound whatever difficulties are present, because they are based on false premises about human psychology and so can only undermine the healthy functioning of the human psyche. I have seen many unhappy people adopt these distorted patterns of living and be further hurt and damaged, victims, in a sense, of those who have promoted these alternate life styles. And finally, I know that people are unfortunately still being actively solicited to participate in such destructive ways of trying to deal with adulthood.

Through this book, which is based on my clinical experience, I hope to save some people from trying to solve their problems by making such destructive choices, and to support healthy people who have no inclination toward such choices, but who are subject to social pressure against marriage. In the chapters that follow, then, I defend and praise marriage—for it is indeed a praiseworthy institution—analyze its difficulties, and discuss how it can be made to work.

Many people have influenced the development of this book and helped with the task of writing it.

If first wish to express my appreciation to my teachers and preceptors at the Mount Sinai Institute of Psychiatry in New York City who trained and taught me how to become a psychiatrist. To the community of the Phelps Memorial Hospital at North Tarrytown, New York, my thanks for accepting me into their fold and giving me the opportunity to work and mature as a psychiatrist.

Special thanks must go to Hunt Cole and Barbara Fried for their superb help in editing the manuscript and to Phyllis Colin, Mimi Finkel, Rhoda Heller, and Debra Tanklow for ther patient help in typing and retyping.

To all of these people and many others, my thanks for your encouragement and support.

JOANNA MAGDA POLENZ, M.D.

In Defense of Marriage

CHAPTER 1

What Marriage Is And Isn't

Marriage has always existed in one form or another in all cultures. It is an agreement and a relationship between two people that offers them a better chance for happiness and fulfillment than any other arrangement. In recent years it has become fashionable to denigrate marriage, and to propose alternate, "freer" styles of relationships between men and women. This book is on the side of marriage, the people who are married, whether for the first or second or whatever time, and those who plan to be married. I hope that what it has to say will help some of them get along better as married couples, not only for their own sakes but also for the sake of their children, the adults of tomorrow. The best gift any married couple can give their children is to get along well with each other, since the firmest foundation for future happiness is to be the child of a happy marriage. Such children are able to form deep and lasting relationships as well as superficial relationships; they are also more optimistic and more able to handle new and varied situations.

I do not mean to put down people who have failed at marriage or who do not find it appealing. Most certainly I do not intend to criticize anyone who chooses a different life style, a different sexual relationship, or a different mode of self-expression. Human nature, upbringing, and later experience are very diverse. We are all very much alike—otherwise the science of human behavior would not be possible—but we are all also very different, so that individuals must find their own solutions to common life problems. On the other hand, because I know that life styles based on sexual nonexclusiveness are unable to provide happiness and fulfillment and are psychologically destructive, it is with sadness that I hear of people undertaking them. I do condemn people who draw into these life styles those who might have found a better way.

Divergent life styles have always been with us. But today they are unusually visible due to the emphasis on diversity and individualism that came to the fore in our society in the 1960s. Their proponents advertise them as superior, and by doing so put down traditional ways. However, the same open-mindedness that advocates of divergent life styles beg for is due also those people who want a conventional marriage—that is, a monogamous sexual relationship containing much to hold the partners together, including a promise to try and make it last forever. Of course many people fail to reach the goals they set for themselves, in marriage as elsewhere.

We are not all beautiful; we are not all wise; we are not all talented or creative. Nor are we consistent. We go through periods when we manage our lives well and periods when we can't seem to manage at all. An undertaking that is tried by most people, as marriage is, and is supposed to last a lifetime should not be expected to have a higher level of success than other human commitments.

Marriage, then, is no panacea and no paradise. It has all the shortcomings and flaws of any other human enterprise, and also reflects the shortcomings of the people who attempt it. Some of us succeed at it the first time; some succeed the second or third time; some try often and never succeed. Success in marriage is not something that always happens to the right people or the good people. A marriage does not come naturally, and is easily wounded.

Once married, we are not automatically made secure. The only marriages that succeed are those in which the partners consider each other's feelings and needs and realize that for their own good and the good of the marriage they must accommodate one another. In short, both partners have to work at making the marriage a success. People who are willing and able to make that kind of effort should be encouraged, because marriage is a proven and rewarding life style that has stood the test of time.

To make a successful marriage, a man or woman must first of all desire marriage enough to make a commitment to it. In a world that allows people many life styles and various kinds of relationships, a person who chooses marriage has to regard it as a very long-term commitment and understand that it precludes other choices. Marriage can work only for those people whose needs it fulfills, who will not feel too deprived by the loss of other possibilities.

WHAT MARRIAGE OFFERS

What marriage offers can be stated quite simply:

1. Marriage is for people who are seeking a long-term, intense relationship with another person, the kind of relationship that promises you the security of feeling you are loved.

2. Marriage is an acknowledged and legally supported forum for sexual pursuit and fulfillment and it promises a sexual relationship built on love and commitment. However, marriage is not the only possible way to achieve a sexual relationship, and it is not suited for a sexual life based on homosexual, bigamous, or group sexual relationships. It is a monogamous, heterosexual relationship.

3. Marriage offers companionship during both the good and the bad times of life. A marriage partner is a companion with whom to share all life's concerns—work, money, home, possessions, adversity, illness, old age, and joy.

4. Marriage seems to make it easier for both partners to devote time and attention to their home.

5. Marriage offers the best possible setting for having and raising children. People certainly can and do raise children outside marriage, but it is always much more difficult.

6. Finally, marriage supports the pursuit of long-term goals. The experience of loving and being loved by a willing, able,

and desired sexual partner in the security and stability of an ongoing relationship frees both partners from instinctual pressures, which in turn gives them the energy to pursue long-term work or intellectual goals, and to master useful and pleasurable skills. Only when we are not lonely, and when our instinctual needs for security, sex, and companionship are satisfied, are we able to invest psychic energy in outside, long-term goals. The great majority of people find that marriage is the best way to relieve the pain of loneliness and to satisfy their instinctual needs.

Before committing ourselves to marriage, we need to ask ourselves whether and how much we are indeed interested in having the things that marriage is most useful for. It's not necessary to want everything marriage offers; for instance, not all adults desire or are suited to be parents, and therefore not all adults, even though married, should have children. The essential question is, "Do I want enough of what marriage can give to make it compellingly right for me?"

If you answer yes to this question, you then need to make an honest appraisal of your own abilities and limitations: "Am I a person who can handle marriage? Is marriage a workable life style for me?" Keep in mind that for all the benefits that marriage offers, it does have drawbacks. It is not an independent endeavor, but a partnership; therefore, from the day of the wedding, your life will be seriously influenced by your spouse. Marriage ties you down to one partner for a long, long time, ideally for life.

Furthermore, marriage is not geared for the pursuit of either recreational activity in general or escapist pleasures in particular as much as it is for the serious ongoing activity of building a life together. When recreation and escape are central preoccupations, the more serious tasks of adulthood are usually neglected. If you try to make marriage a round of fun, fun, fun! it is very apt to collapse.

CRITICISMS OF MARRIAGE

Marriage, then, is ideally both exclusive and permanent. Both these ideals have lately been attacked as being too constraining and psychologically unhealthy. Critics of marriage are against the bond between husband and wife and also against the special privileges they extend to one another. If there were no husbands and wives, they say, men would tend to treat all women, and women would tend to treat all men the same way—intensely, passionately, and with consideration—so that there would be more happiness for everybody and fewer lonely and unhappy people. But however appealing this argument may be, the assumption that it's based on is false.

Criticisms of marriage of course reflect what is going on in our society at large. Our culture now permits more choices in many areas of life—where and how people live, their work and recreation, how they dress, their religious practices, their styles of life—that are far freer than the choices permitted even twenty years ago. This new freedom has led people to experiment with new and unusual personal life styles. Some of the experimentation has proven to be energizing and healthy; some of it has made many people feel lonely, alienated, and confused, especially those unable to find in life the choices they have been led to expect.

It is also true that old forms of social order and relationships, particularly the stable, central family group, have become weaker. The mobility demanded by our society—for instance, the frequency with which employees are required to move—tends to make our personal relationships casual and haphazard. People who can adapt to immediate intimacy are considered to be well adjusted. But all this mobility, this demand for quick relationships does tend to make us feel that everything is dispensable. We can be replaced, and so can any set of friends, any set of neighbors, any set of co-workers.

A superficial openness may be helpful in making new relationships easily, but those who are most easily able to adapt to quick intimacy are also most apt to suffer from deep feelings of loneliness and alienation. If they are married, they may blame these feelings on their marriage, instead of on the real cause, the isolating qualities of modern life. They may start to look restlessly for something else.

That something else may range from pickups in singles bars for instant sexual intimacy; to people who barely know one another establishing a household and living together with little planning or thought to the meaning of such arrangements or the consequences to either or both partners; to pairs of married couples swinging—that is, trading partners with out all living together—to small or large group marriages in communal quarters. Some swinging arrangements and communes involve actual group sex, some don't. Also, now that it has become more possible for homosexuals and heterosexuals to mix socially, some swinging and communal sexual arrangements have started to include homosexuality and bisexuality. Homosexual arrangements may also be resorted to by lonely people in communes and elsewhere, when no heterosexual partner is available, as an easy way to avoid having to find or attract an appropriate heterosexual partner.

I've already said that the rationale for doing away with marriage is based on a false assumption—namely, that people would offer the same special consideration they give to their spouses to many more people. Communal arrangements are also based on false premises, that all people ought to be loved equally and all relationships ought to be considered equally good. If all relationships are equally good, they should all be alike; activities should not be restricted to certain people in special relationships because that means those relationships are more privileged and others are denigrated. Ultimately this means that people themselves do not matter at all; the only thing that counts is what you do with them. You don't feel more love for everyone, but only a kind of spurious intimacy with strangers. The communal rhetoric preaches general social egalitarianism—absolutely equal sharing of money and household jobs, for instance. The communal life style thus comes to encompass all of personal life. This egalitarianism tends to squelch individuality and specialness in areas other than intimate relations, and makes the commune a hard, impersonal institution.

Most people sense the difficulty and pain that are part of all these alternative relationships and do not adopt them. But many others, especially those people who are unsettled, lost, or depressed, do adopt them, and do great damage to themselves. A person, for example, who is basically heterosexual but who hasn't yet achieved a clear sense of that identity will have more trouble doing so if he or she becomes involved in homosexual activity, or a person who is on the edge of a deep depression may topple into depression if he or she spends much time in the personally unsupportive atmosphere of singles bars.

THE STRENGTHS OF MARRIAGE

The fact is that the strong bond formed by exclusiveness and permanence is exactly what gives such strength and magic to the institution of marriage. Maybe it is difficult not to break this bond—not to betray it, not to cheat; but the two people in a marriage do know they are special, precious, and indeed necessary to each other, and so they make the effort.

They do so for a profound psychological reason. Every human being longs for a close and intimate, maybe even unrealistically close and intimate, relationship with someone else. This desire is based on the nature of human development. A baby is born helpless, dependent for its survival on the good will of the adults around it, especially its mother. The infant responds with intense love for its mother, who responds to the child's emotion with augmented love of her own. This intense one-to-one relationship is uniquely satisfying and fulfilling, and it serves as the prototype for all the child's future relationships. Everyone who has had it always seeks to establish something like it again, and even those who did not have an entirely satisfactory relationship with their mothers still want something like what they had or needed as children.

Later in life sexual attraction brings this desire for an intense relationship into full and joyous consciousness. Marriage endures simply because it offers us the best chance to fulfill, however imperfectly or incompletely, our ever-present dream of once again being totally loved and accepted.

Marriages fail when people are too damaged to be able to achieve fulfillment of these desires. Many find the challenge difficult and demanding, especially when the desired exclusiveness must be considered permanent. Nonetheless, they continue to seek an intense relationship, because, like everybody else, they too started as infants.

Because the relationship between a baby and its mother is so intense, a toddler who is being displaced by a newborn sibling and has to learn to share the mother is bound to suffer frustration and grief. This sharing relationship is the prototype for the communal relationships proposed as alternatives to marriage. Communes resemble a sibship—several women, several men, no envy, no specialness, no jealousy, no exclusiveness. Everybody is included, nobody is excluded. The only problem is that communal relationships simply don't work. They do not give happiness. They do not elicit feelings of acceptance and love. Rather, they provoke a feeling of nothingness, of emptiness. People drift or turn away from the communal setting because it does not give them the intense exclusive relationship they want.

Ironically, many marriages fail because the partners want not wisely but too well. They overidealize the possibilities in their marriage. They try to always be together or they try to be always aware of each other. In a word, they try to recreate the intense childish relationship between infant and mother too completely. They do not have enough maturity to develop a relationship with adult vitality and freshness.

Extralegal alternatives to marriage also do not work as well as a legal marriage. If a couple said to me, "We don't want to marry legally, but we love each other and we'll live together and be faithful forever," I would certainly wish them well; but they would have to be quite special people to make a success of their effort. Such a relationship is harder to manage than a legal marriage. Ambivalence is present in everyone; we all have mixed emotions, which often provoke suspicions and doubt about each other, feelings that are more apt to grow when there are no legal constraints on the relationship. We all also tend to be more or less impulsive, so that we are apt to flirt, to be faithless, to put money into shaky investments, to do countless things that can cause deep emotional or practical damage to a love relationship. Legal liability helps to make us think ahead. Furthermore, many social facts of life make the legal bond useful. Why not use it? Why force children to suffer the slights that are always offered to people born illegitimately? Indeed, why not take all the psychological and social help the law provides? A legal marriage is the best setting for an exclusive, permanent sexual relationship; it offers the most security and the most support, all of which may at some time be crucial.

Most people realize this. That's why many divorcees are barely out of one marriage before they start looking for another marital partner, and also why our society has adjusted its customs to enable them to remarry without stigma. Indeed, all cultures have understood the benefits of marriage, including its importance to the continuation of the culture itself. That is why all societies support marriage, why they try to sustain a legal setting in which good will and common interests can exist between the partners. In every culture laws not only establish but also actively support marriage.

Marriage thus joins two people who have found and chosen each other out of the vast pool of the inhabitants of this earth, who consider each other to be impressive, desirable, lovable. They pool their resources—physical, psychological, emotional, financial, intellectual—and start building a new life together, working together and helping one another. It is a liberating, not a constricting situation. They share some of the tasks of life, leaving each one of them more energy and time for other activities, other interests, further growth. And they know that their relationship is supported and approved by their society, for the social structure itself depends on the stability of the family.

CHAPTER 2

Stress on Marriage

When our success and contentment depend on another person, as they do in marriage, any time the other person feels stressed or frightened, shaken or insecure, we ourselves also tend to feel frightened, shaken, and insecure almost at once. This marital contagion of stress can be a serious matter. Human life being what it is, we don't have to go looking for emotional troubles because sooner or later we'll have our share, sooner or later we are bound to experience stress. A person in stress feels uncomfortable, unhappy, and discontented, and wants whatever is wrong at the moment to get better as soon as possible.

When a married person is going through a difficult, stressful time, usually the marriage is stressed too. Stress can have positive as well as negative effects on a marriage. Devastating misfortunes can cause even a strong, stable, and satisfying marriage to crumble. On the other hand, marital partners who come through a period of stress successfully will know they have an inner strength; this knowledge leads them to expect that they will solve future problems, too. Their marriage thus becomes firmer, and they are more confident that it will survive.

Successfully overcoming stress together does indeed enrich the marital experience; however, this does not mean you should find or create problems as a way of strengthening your marriage. When you provoke something, you often precipitate a situation that is beyond handling. Stress is a very draining experience, and it affects everything in a marriage; how the marital partners respond to each other, how they work, take care of the home, take care of the children—in short, how they function.

The list of potential hardships and disasters ranges from universal events like war, political upheaval, and economic depression, through earthquake and flood, to purely personal difficulties, such as illness, death, lost friendships, or lost prestige. Although such experiences are universal, we react to them as individuals, so that the very same dreadful experience will affect individuals differently. Our reactions to relatively ordinary, daily stress are even more personal, because they are determined to an even greater extent by our internal reality and to a lesser extent by the external reality of our surroundings.

Internal reality is our personal view of the world; it affects any and all of our life situations. This inner view is to some extent symbolic: we make things in the real world stand for the events or people of our inner reality—important previous experiences, and particularly previous conflicts between instinctual needs and desires and external reality. These old conflicts involve parents or other authority figures such as teachers, siblings, and sometimes even friends. They may have been open struggles or muted difficulties. If an early conflict is not successfully resolved, we push it out of our awareness, but we may unconsciously attach its stresses to something in the present environment and experience this piece of the present as stressful in itself.

UNRESOLVED EARLY STRESS

Stress based on old unresolved conflicts does not usually dominate our lives; nonetheless we must be aware that many real-life events we experience as stressful are perceived that way because we use them as symbols of old struggles. This is especially likely to be true when we feel unhappy or anxious in a situation where other people are comfortable. This kind of stress can be very serious, even debilitating. Although it may not be realistic, living with it can be just as wearying as living through the most obvious kind of disaster. It is a psychologically complex event; we are trying to resolve an old conflict in a present context. When the present context is a marriage and one or both partners use the events of married life symbolically, it can produce much trouble. Even trivial daily events can begin to take up an unreasonable amount of time, energy, and/or money.

The fact is, we do things because of unconscious motivations–transposed, camouflaged desires to win the attention, love, and praise of key figures from our childhood, whose love we either were not able to win or thought we had not won. That is why we often do things that alienate us from the people who now provide us with sustenance and affection. We are still trying to win the love of the parents of our childhood, and by doing so we may be robbing ourselves of the possibility of having love now.

Take George, for example, a successful businessman, father of three, who spends many hours working for the benefit of his family–a realistic necessity in his field of work. On the weekend he spends his time jogging, bicycling, and playing tennis. He boasts with inordinate pleasure about how great his body is and how his tennis game has improved. In the meantime, his wife is lonely and his children–two boys and a girl–never see him. He loves them, he says. He wants them to do well at school, but he never has time to go over their homework with them, never has time to ask what they're reading, or if they're reading at all.

George's father was a gym teacher. George was a fine boy who did quite well at school. He was only a mediocre athlete, though, much to his father's disappointment, who wanted to be able to boast about George and show him off as a sign of his own success as a gym teacher. Despite his rather unsatisfactory relationship with his father, George has become successful. He has overcome the handicap of his father's disappointment, and what George perceived as his father's rejection and lack of love and appreciation. Now, as an adult, he is athletic far more than he needs to be to stay healthy or even be in good shape. Though he doesn't know it, he's still trying to earn love and praise through athletic success. He's unaware that although he wants approval, acceptance, and love, he's pushing away his wife and children, the people who want most to give him those very things.

Or, take Marion, a very attractive woman, married to her high school sweetheart, mother of two children, a boy eight and a girl five. She was a vivacious and popular girl whose mother, although she loved her daughter, was jealous of her. Because of her angry envy, the mother would fight with Marion especially about social events, call her a slut, and tell her that her messy room and untidy books absolutely proved that both her behavior and her morals were questionable. Now, Marion is a fanatic housekeeper. She is still trying to prove to her mother that she is a good, moral, and worthwhile person. She spends immense amounts of time and energy cleaning her house, leaving herself exhausted and drained, and much too tired for sex, so that she can consider herself a clean girl worthy of her mother's love.

Consider, also, Richard, a professional man who is married to a school teacher. They have two young children. The family is well off with two incomes, but they do very little because he insists that they have no money. His father was a gambler. They were extremely poor, and they never did anything pleasurable together. He always promised himself that when he was grown up and the head of a family, things would be different, but they aren't. He still acts as though he's poor. He was so hurt by the early poverty and insecurity that he can't get over it. He has to hold on to all their earnings in an effort to heal the early wounds of his childhood.

What a person finds stressful comes out of the struggle of the personality to find its identity and come to peace with the tribulations of life. It's wrong, therefore, to belittle or to criticize a spouse for finding certain things difficult, frightening, or unbearable. If you do not give him or her support but rather sit in judgment, you will rob him or her of both peace and identity. "You should not be afraid of my intellectual friends just because you don't have as much education." "You should not be made anxious by my living on credit, it's fun." "You should not be upset by my sexual preferences even if they are different from yours." "You should not be afraid of flying, I'm not." These statements attack the spouse's individuality, point of view, idiosyncrasies,—all the personal preferences we are all entitled to.

Belittling the importance of your spouse's anxiety amounts to an attack. When you insist that your partner change to prove love, it's an attack and a rejection. People should not marry to change other people. They should marry to live with them, which means accepting them. Any change that occurs must be due, not to the other's demand, but to an internal desire for change. Therefore, even if you don't understand or approve of your spouse's anxiety, you should support him or her at the time it's acute. When it's not so acute, you can say how the stress affects you, and how you would like to help your spouse see it differently, particularly if you're also willing to see it from the other point of view yourself. That is not a rejection. But it should not be done when your partner is going through the worst time, and it should be done only with the *hope* of producing change, not with the ultimatum, "You either stop all this or else." Ultimatums are not conducive to a happy marriage.

UNCONSCIOUS NEEDS

Another kind of stress is caused by the fact that we make many of our choices—about work, possessions, life style—because we are driven to do so by our unconscious needs. As a result, some life choices may turn out to be problematic.

Some of us, because of quirks and conflicts in our personalities, crave most the things that terrify and can hurt us. A very shy person becomes an actor or enters politics. It is usually unconscious motivation that drives people to produce beyond their capacity. An unreasonable drive fueled by unconscious motivation in any area—to make money, to excel in work, to excel in sports, to be a social success and leader, to be a civic leader—can hurt a marriage badly. Some people are so driven, so disgusted by their own limitations that they esteem only that which is beyond what they can do and therefore damaging to them. They crave to achieve those things to the exclusion of other needs and at the expense of other legitimate drives.

For instance, take Bill—a forty-seven-year-old successful lawyer, a partner in a prominent firm. He should be very happy. He has professional success, money, an attractive wife, and healthy, vigorous children. Yet there is something restless about Bill. He gives the impression that wherever he is, he would rather be somewhere else. He works hard, very hard; he is always reassuring himself and promising his family that soon he'll stop, but his life has always been like that. He used to say, "When I get into law school." Then it was, "When I finish law school"—"when I pass the bar exams"—"when I make partner"—"when I make senior partner"—"when we have a house." Now he has two houses, other investments, and substantial security, and he's still working just as hard, often to a point of exhaustion. Now he says, "after I finish this particular case," "this particular commitment," "this particular piece of work," but he always finds one more court case, one more commitment, one more pressing piece of work.

His family clamors for attention at home, and he promises to vacation with them, but then he has to cut it short and get back to the office. Or else he brings work on vacation, and gets very angry when the family interrupts him.

Why is Bill so driven? He was a good-looking, smart boy and he was his mother's favorite. She was from a prominent family, and her favorite brother was a successful judge. Bill's father was a real estate salesman. He did all right, but he never equaled the success or prestige of Bill's uncle, the judge. Bill knew that his mother esteemed his uncle, and that she wanted his father to be more like him. When that didn't work out, she pinned her hopes on Bill. Bill never could and still can't take any chance of losing her love, which he equates with losing her esteem. Even though she's dead, Bill is still afraid that if he stops winning new honors and new successes, somehow he will lose his mother's good opinion. Bill knows he's tense, that he can't relax, and that he doesn't feel well. He's aware that he's not as happy as he thinks he should be, and definitely not as happy as he thought he would be. He has trouble sleeping and needs two drinks, sometimes more, before he goes to bed. He's a little concerned about becoming dependent on alcohol, but he will do anything to keep going rather than disappoint his mother.

Helen, on the other hand, feels life is only worthwhile when she's having fun. She's a thirty-six-year-old housewife and mother of three. Fun to Helen means going out Friday, Saturday, and maybe Sunday, as well as on a night or two during the week. By going out Helen means getting dressed up, having dinner in a restaurant, and going to the theater, or better still, going dancing. Her husband is an insurance salesman. He works hard and often has to work evenings. He likes to be at home when he's not working, be with his children, help with their homework, play with them, and attend to chores around the house. He likes to go out with his wife, but he also likes recreation that includes the whole family. He likes to go dancing with Helen, but he'd rather do it occasionally. Helen, however, insists that they don't do enough fun things. If she doesn't get her way, she becomes angry, even abusive and then turns despondent.

Why is this so? Helen can be very reasonable; she loves her husband, and she wants them to have a good life together. She loves the children and can be a very sensitive and attentive mother. Her background explains her behavior. Her mother was young and beautiful when Helen was a little girl. She went out a lot, no matter how much her children cried or were unhappy. She didn't always arrange for someone to care for them while she was away. Helen remembers her mother as pretty, as smelling good and looking happy and cheerful when she went out. Helen loved her mother most the way she looked when she was going out, because Helen also remembers that when her mother was home she wasn't always so pretty, she didn't always dress so nicely or smell so good, and she certainly wasn't sweet, cheerful, or patient. What Helen wants so desperately to achieve through going out is not really an evening of recreation with her husband, but to be with her young beautiful mother as she imagines her mother must have been on those mysterious evenings when she went out.

Other people need stress. They are only able to tolerate a relationship, including a marital relationship, when it is surrounded by crises. They go through life looking for disasters and pain, so that they can feel alive, or indeed feel at all. They often tempt fate, which obligingly is apt to provide them with tragedy; the point is that only in times of stress are they able to function. When these people get married they simply cannot stand a peaceful existence. They make trouble because, for them, the marriage is not successful unless it is a constant struggle with disaster or at least with some demanding project. They are able to turn one of the most desirable aspects of a marriage—the chance to enjoy a stable, contented relationship on an ongoing basis—into a disadvantage. For instance, some people develop what is called "secondary gain" from an illness and do not cooperate with their physician as much as they should to get well because they feel that this adversity is necessary to keep their marriage going.

Laura, for example, was the youngest of four children. By the time she was born, her parents were elderly, and her next youngest sibling was eight years old. The parents doted on Laura. She was their toy. The other children were expected to behave as responsible members of the family, with chores and other appropriate duties, while Laura was exempt. Her middle-aged mother hovered over her, panic-stricken at any sign of illness. She kept the child at home and pampered her shamelessly, giving in to her every whim.

Illness was a fun time for Laura, because she soon discovered that sickness was an excellent excuse for not going to school when she didn't want to. Illness became her friend, a way out of trouble. The other children were chastised for not doing their chores or not taking responsibilities seriously, for being selfish, lazy, or undependable. Laura never was chastised.

Although she frequently seemed ill, in reality she was quite a healthy girl who grew into a sturdy if not very pretty woman and married a somewhat insecure man fifteen years older, for whom she became a "child bride." He found her apparent frailty most attractive. It made him feel more important and more secure. He simply took over where Laura's mother had left off. Laura managed to have two children, both of whom are also apparently quite sickly. They both have had their tonsils and adenoids out because Laura insisted they were always sick with sore throats, although it took some time before she convinced the doctor to perform the operations. So far, they've managed to retain their appendices. However, Laura is always saying with some pride that they're frail children, and if there's anything going around, they'll get it.

Laura has had a hysterectomy. It was not quite clear that she really needed it, but she finally found a doctor whom she was able to convince that her periods were hemorrhages accompanied by excruciating pain, so that she was becoming totally debilitated. At the age of twenty-five, after the birth of her first child, she developed chronic, incapacitating back pain. Bed rest, hospitalization, traction, muscle relaxants, and tranquilizers did not help. Finally, when she was thirty-two, she underwent back surgery, a spinal fusion, which was only marginally successful. Furthermore, Laura's gall bladder is beginning to act up, so that she suffers indigestion and pain after rich meals.

Her husband is most devoted. Of course he has not done very well at his job; after all, he has a sick wife and is not able to devote himself wholeheartedly to his career. Surprisingly, he does not seem to mind. He is very supportive and not at all resentful of Laura and her many illnesses. It may be, of course, that he's rather grateful to her because he never did believe that he could be a success and Laura's illness gives him an excuse not to have to face his limitations. Laura also has taken her illnesses with incredible courage. She is quite cheerful, and talks at length about her many doctors, almost as if she enjoys her pain. Indeed, her illnesses have been the central activity of her life. She's never tried to find a job outside her home, and needs a great deal of help taking care of her children. Her husband has certainly not developed any interests outside the home; after all, his wife is a sick woman, and he's needed there. He feels important, and he also has an excuse for all his failings. He likes Laura to be at home so he always knows where she is.

What are the consequences of this situation, which will probably go on indefinitely since it fulfills so many of their needs? The real consequences are dire. Their financial situation is shaky. They've had horrendous medical bills. Laura's husband has had to change jobs because her illnesses have kept him out of work so often. They have also had to move many times, looking for the perfect climate for Laura and the children. These are only some of the consequences of their maladaptive adjustment to reality and their enjoyment of what most people would consider serious adversity.

DEALING WITH STRESS

Stress is contagious, as I said above, and present in all relationships. The only appropriate way to deal with it is to accept it and cope with it rationally. You have to understand how it is that you get caught up in it, and find out if it's an appropriate reaction in your own situation. If you are extremely frightened by what you are feeling, you may need psychiatric help.

The better put together you are, the better you'll be able to protect yourself from emotional contagion in a marriage. The signs of a well-put-together person are that you have a clear picture of yourself; you're aware of whom you are, where you come from, and where you hope to be going; and you can function well at a job and in your free time. But even if you're in very good psychological shape, you are apt to be somewhat frightened if your spouse feels anxious or stressed. That means you may become impatient and abrupt with your spouse, and that is certainly not helpful.

It is easier to empathize and be helpful when you can identify with the feeling of stress; that is, you also find his or her situation stressful. Disaster is easiest of all to empathize with because it is universal; it is much more difficult to be supportive when the circumstances are such that they would not make you anxious. And without the ability to empathize and therefore share the anxiety or at least to understand it, it is difficult to be around people under stress. They are suspicious, quarrelsome, depressed, and anxious, without vigor or confidence. They transmit anxiety and evoke anger. They behave childishly; they are preoccupied with themselves; they exhibit nervous mannerisms and habits that under more favorable circumstances they are able to control. When the person to whom you are married begins to act like this, it's not only frightening, it's also extremely unpleasant. Consequently, you may react in an unpleasant, even ugly way.

It is hard to be gentle and supportive; sometimes it's impossible—if your spouse is behaving in a way that you find not only incomprehensible but obnoxious, abhorrent, or shameful. It's also difficult to be supportive if your spouse reacts with anxiety to something—say, travel—that you find desirable or even essential to a good life.

Take, as an example, David and Mary, who have been married for fifteen years. They met in college. David was a football player. He seemed fun-loving, outgoing, and carefree, characteristics that attracted Mary. Mary saw herself as a timid person, shy and afraid of new situations, and she found David supportive and reassuring. After they were married, Mary realized that David had been at his very best in college, where he felt financially secure because his parents were able to put him through school and he didn't have to work. During their married life, making a living has turned out to be David's greatest challenge and one that he finds frightening.

At age forty, David has recently been promoted to Regional Sales Manager, with an increase in salary, but he does not behave in a way appropriate to a man who's just had a stroke of good fortune. He looks sad and frightened. He's neither physically affectionate to his wife nor does he joke with her. Actually, it's difficult for her even to have a conversation with him, and he's mean to the children.

Mary sees no reason for this behavior. She would like to enjoy their good fortune, go out more, and enjoy their greater financial security. But if she suggests having friends over to celebrate, David shouts at her, refuses to participate and even refuses to allow her to plan such an event. He has trouble sleeping and eating, and his interest in sex has markedly decreased.

David is still able to function on his job. In spite of his morose behavior at home, he is able to get up in the morning, shave, dress in a clean and appropriate fashion, and leave for work. On weekends, however, he doesn't shave, wash, or even brush his teeth; he just sits in front of the television set and picks his nose.

Actually David is good with people and, when not frightened, he can even act like a leader. Once he gets used to his new job, his mood will improve, his anxiety will decrease, he will pay attention to Mary and the children, and start washing and shaving on weekends. Luckily David only becomes this frightened and incapacitated when he faces a major change. He has learned to handle daily ups and downs of the working world quite well, so that Mary, who's been through this before, knows that the worst will soon be over. Consequently she is able to support and sympathize with his temporary acute incapacity, although David, the working man, has never been as much fun as David, the college man.

It's both difficult and draining if one partner gets tense frequently or is usually tense; often the anxiety is simply too expensive in emotional energy for the marriage to continue. It simply may not be healthy or wise for the unstressed partner to continue to try to sustain the spouse. The emotional burden may be so tremendous and demand such denial of the unstressed spouse's desires, interests, and ideas that the marriage is not worth the effort it takes to maintain it.

One such marriage was Carl and Eleanor's. They met when he was a graduate student and she was an undergraduate. Carl was a very serious scholar of history who didn't have much of a social life and didn't know anything about women except that he felt shy and awkward with them. When he fell in love with Eleanor, he loved being in love, and, after only a very short courtship, they were married because he wanted to return to the serious pursuit of his studies.

After they were married, Carl was quite surprised by Eleanor. Since she was quiet, withdrawn, and did not have many boy friends, he anticipated that she would be grateful for his attentions forever. As soon as she became his wife, her temperament changed. She became demanding, loud, and not easy to satisfy. She wanted a lot of help from Carl with the housework, even though she had reduced her courses to devote more of her time to being a wife. Carl was carrying a heavy graduate schedule and was also working as a teaching assistant, but he did try to help around the house. He believed in equal rights, but he was somewhat taken aback by the fact that Eleanor never managed to get her share of the housework done; furthermore, what she did was always slipshod while she demanded that his share be finished to perfection. She complained about where and how they lived, and when he tried to fix up their house and make it more attractive, she complained that he was neglecting her and not spending enough time with her. She complained about their sex life, and about his insensitivity. No matter how hard he tried to please, nothing worked.

Carl felt very unhappy about all this, but accepted a great deal of the blame, because he knew so little about women. His self-esteem was not high, and he often felt insecure and inadequate; he was therefore willing to believe that Eleanor had a realistic basis for her complaints. Their courtship had been so short and he had been so delighted with Eleanor that he had overlooked or ignored what he should have seen. He had not realized, for instance, that Eleanor, who was an only child, was always going home because she needed an enormous amount of support, reassurance, and sustenance from her parents, and that she was only able to function in school because she had good, consistent, and frequent psychiatric treatment. Eleanor, in fact, was deeply troubled, overwhelmed by feelings of inadequacy and lack of self-worth, and terrified of almost everything. Because she was so tortured and drained by her ruminations and obsessions, she took out her frustration and misery on the one person with whom she felt comfortable, Carl.

Another example of this kind of stressful situation is the marriage of Margot and Ed. Margot is twenty-eight, an accountant with a good job. She had never been very successful socially since first study, and then work had taken most of her time. She met Ed at a party. He was thirty-four, and worked in his father's business. He seemed very strong, and talked a lot about business deals and traveling, all of which Margot found appealing. He asked for her phone number and called the next day and, after a short courtship, they were married. They spent most of their courtship planning their wedding trip, a tour through Europe.

Margot knew something was wrong on her wedding day when Ed showed up drunk. They had planned to leave for Paris the next day but, when he woke up, Ed wasn't so sure it was such a good idea. Maybe he ought not to leave his father to handle the business all by himself; should they take the risk of flying? And was it such a good idea to go to Europe after all? They did go on their wedding trip but it wasn't what Margot had expected. Ed's moods fluctuated from day to day. In the evening he would seem buoyant, alive, and full of ideas. The next morning, however, he was full of doubts and insecurity and indecision. By the time their wedding trip was over, Margot knew that she had married a man with serious psychological problems, and knew that a lot of her energy, time, and effort would have to be spent helping him.

Margot also realized she had to make a decision. She had to decide how much she was committed to Ed and how much she loved him, and whether his good qualities—his intelligence, imagination, and loyalty—were enough to compensate her for the consequences of living with a man whose problems were so extensive.

Marriages where one partner's stress is just too hard for the other to deal with may arise when the partners lack awareness of self or of the other person; when the two have a mutual misunderstanding about each other; or when one of the two is plain dishonest. Most of these mistakes are made during courtship, when people tend to cover up their faults and try to present only the attractive aspects of their personalities. Courtship itself often makes people so eager to wed that they are willing to overlook shortcomings and incompatibilities that, later on, they will no longer put up with or accept. During courtship, of course, couples are usually not exposed to circumstances that precipitate a stress reaction, so it is not easy to learn how and why the partner is made anxious, and whether their thresholds for stress are compatible. Furthermore, a threshold for stress may change during marriage because of external circumstances or problems. When either partner's response to stress becomes simply unbearable and impossible for the other partner to handle, the marriage may no longer be viable.

CHAPTER 3

Sex and Marriage

THE SEXUAL ADVANTAGES OF MARRIAGE

By and large, adults who have an active sex life are happier than adults who don't. Sexual fulfillment makes us feel relaxed and content. It is good for self-esteem. It releases a great deal of instinctual energy, so that good sex leaves a person refreshed and ready to deal with life's other commitments. One of the basic advantages of marriage is that it is an excellent setting for relaxed, comfortable, and frequent sex.

The sex act can be an act of great love, of intense tenderness, of much understanding between two people, or it can be a sensual experience just for a fleeting moment—nothing but the touching of two skins. It can also be an act of aggression, a frightening, even traumatizing, demeaning assault. The very same act performed by the very same organs can be any one of these things.

The way sex is experienced depends on the characteristics of the circumstances in which it occurs. Most important of these characteristics is the relationship that exists between the people having it; this relationship has by far the greatest influence on the sex act, what it signifies, and how it is experienced. And the complicated, multidimensional relationship of marriage turns out to be very good for sex.

Both the selection of a mate and the contractual arrangement that are part of marriage have certain practical elements that are helpful to the sexual experience. You have the opportunity during courtship to choose a partner carefully; your contract with each other is permanent. Single people have to spend much time and energy seeking sexual partners; married people have the great advantage of knowing they have a sexual partner at home who will be there no matter what.

Another most important advantage of marriage to sexual fulfillment is psychological. People must feel secure and relaxed to have good sex, and marriage is structured to provide a partner with whom you feel secure and a setting in which you feel safe, so that you can relax.

All the cultural rules that govern everyday behavior are suspended for sex. Normally we leave some distance between ourselves and another human being. We don't sniff or touch each other; we spend much time, effort, and money to present a pleasant, deodorized, and inoffensive facade. We encourage and teach our children from an early age not to stare at other people, and not to discuss other people's physical attributes in front of them.

In sexual activity there is close body contact. Two people touch, feel, kiss, smell one another, and talk about each other's appearance. It is all right to touch and peer into every orifice. There is a mingling of secretions and odors. This abandon is in direct contrast to every other contact that our culture allows.

The behavior that is necessary for a successful sexual experience is thus intimate, open, inquisitive. It is behavior that, for most of us, can most easily be exhibited only when we feel secure and relaxed—that is, when we are with someone we can trust. Trust generally requires continuation and stability, both of which are built into marriage.

There are people for whom this degree of abandon is only possible in exactly the opposite situation—that is, they feel most secure in one-night stands. This may seem paradoxical but it isn't for them; for them, total anonymity provides the still necessary emotional security because only with someone who will stay a stranger are they free to enjoy sex. Such people are not able to form relationships; they fear being loved, they fear loving, or worse, they feel unlovable and therefore apt to think anyone who gets to know them will reject them. They are only hiding their problems from themselves when they brag about their sophistication and think of themselves as being sexually curious and free. Their kind of emotional security brings them no emotion, let alone security, since it exposes them to the possibility of great physical danger. There are no manners in the sex act and you are naked and unprotected with an unknown person whose state of health and sexual preferences are also unknown.

Most people want to conform to the rules of their culture and get satisfaction from knowing they are functioning within those rules; and most people want their sexual activities to be sanctioned and above board. Marriage has a great advantage—it is socially approved for sex. The security of marriage includes having a sexual partner always available—it is an island of peace in a sea of constant searching for achievement and fulfillment. When you're married, your partner is indeed yours, bound to you not only by a personal promise but also by all the weight of society with its laws and pressures.

We have heard much recently about the problems of the monogamous marriage and how it deprives us of adventure and pleasure. But for many people the very promise to be faithful alleviates worry about sexual fidelity; such worry can be a major source of tension and unhappiness. For these people, monogamy brings greater freedom than so-called sexual liberation.

Florence's history, for example, indicates that, for her as for many others, the institution of marriage may be considered necessary for a good sex life. She is an attractive woman of forty-five, married for the second time. She was the older of two children. Her parents were poor and set high standards for the education and achievement of their children. Florence suspects that they had an active sex life since they were openly affectionate to one another; she also suspects that one or both were unfaithful, since she remembers them quarreling.

Florence met her first husband at work. He was older and was separated from his wife. She fell very much in love with him, they started an affair, and their sex was good. She wanted to be his wife both because she loved him and also because she wanted the permanence, stability, and respectability that marriage provides. She ignored his rather obvious faults—vanity, selfishness, impulsiveness, and a desire for self-gratification regardless of cost. When they got married, the sex for her became great. They had, however, many other problems. His needs and his pleasures came before anything else; everything he wanted had to be the best quality, and he didn't care what this meant for the rest of the family. They had three children. After a while, he started to drink and became brutal. For several years things grew progressively harder and Florence really could not understand why she stayed with him. She was still an attractive woman and had affairs with other men; however, the sex with them was always inferior to the sex with her husband. She felt they had some very special sexual bond which was the main reason she put up with him. Eventually, she left him. Although, as a single woman, she had boyfriends and was sexually active, these affairs were not as enjoyable for her as her sex life with her husband had been. She thought that he was unique until she married again—this time to someone who loved her, was good to her children, and was kind, giving, and supportive. She was amazed at how good their sex became after marriage and she finally felt liberated from the hold her first husband had had on her. Florence obviously felt that the best sex only happens between a man and a woman who are deeply committed to each other.

One final sexual advantage of marriage lies in its continuity. All of us are trapped by time and biology. Life moves relentlessly onward and the beauty of youth passes for all of us. Our sexual desires continue right through life. It has been proven that the most important factor in staying sexually active for a long time is the ready availability of a suitable and willing partner; marriage makes it possible. Long after youth has gone, when the skin is no longer smooth and the muscles are no longer taut—for both of you—the marital relationship endures.

POSSIBLE SEXUAL PROBLEMS

Separation. Since sex is one of the basic reasons for getting married, when things go wrong with sex, the marriage is in trouble. Sex becomes a problem if there is too little of it. What amount of sex is too little is a personal standard. Medical data may indicate where the majority of people fall, what the median is, what the average is; the amount of sex that is right for particular people, however, is what makes them content. Too little means too little to feel satisfied; having a sense of deprivation, a feeling of not having enough.

While sexual fulfillment is certainly basic to a good life, life presents many situations where it isn't possible. A job, for example, may sometimes require long separations or one partner may become ill.

Fred and Jane present a typical problem of separation. They have had a passionate relationship since they met in law school. They have lived together since they were students, went to the same school, took the same classes, spent practically all their time together. They were accustomed to sleeping and eating together and also depended on one another for support, intellectual stimulation, and validation of their points of view. Each found a good job with a prestigious law firm, but since their work requires a lot of traveling, they are now separated a great deal. They find this very hard. Although their careers are developing as they had hoped, they now must face substantial pressure because of repeated separations. Consequently they must decide if their marriage can continue to function as successfully under these new circumstances. What will it mean to their sex life? Should they put their careers ahead of personal considerations, or should they review what the separations are doing to them as a couple and consider whether one or the other—or both—should change jobs? The stress on the marriage in such a situation is real although the partners may not react to it to the same degree; still, assuming theirs is a reasonably healthy marriage sexually, both partners will suffer some stress of sexual deprivation. How they handle it is a good measure of how strong and durable the bond is between them.

Many suggestions have been offered on how to deal with sexual deprivation, from sublimation—that is, diverting sexual energies into other channels—to self-stimulation, to finding substitute sexual partners. Each couple will find something that is acceptable to them. But, by and large, what will be most helpful to the marriage is to sustain the dedication of the spouses to each other and to the monogamous bond. This means that the couple, out of their devotion to one another, will do without sex, and try to find a substitute for it in other activities.

Although the need for sex is biological, fulfillment can be postponed indefinitely if the individual so chooses. It is a hardship for people who ordinarily have an active sex life to forgo sexual activity for a long time. They will be less enthusiastic about life and less vigorous. They will feel disgruntled and unfulfilled. But it's possible to live this way. Going without sex for a while is not like being deprived of food or water, sleep or breath. We can indeed get along without sexual activity and release. For people who are used to having sex, abstinence is not comfortable; but it is, for them as for consistently sexually deprived people, possible. If abstinence is unacceptable to a couple, they must find other means of coping.

The next best choice for some is masturbation, which at least keeps people monogamous. Many people, however, think masturbation is unappetizing and unfulfilling, and some even think it is psychologically impossible. In general, men find it easier to resort to masturbation than women. Some people cannot accept it because they believe the old wives' tale that it makes you go crazy. Many more just find it so unattractive that they don't even consider using it as an outlet when they are sexually deprived. Almost everyone will agree that it is inferior to intercourse, and actually people who prefer masturbation to sex with another person do have problems that sexual contact activates. Masturbation is not in itself harmful, and if it helps people through a period of sexual deprivation, fine and good. However, some people do feel that masturbation is disloyal to a spouse, and if such a person discovers that his or her spouse engaged in masturbation, it's taken as a betrayal and a sexual transgression against themselves.

It is a mistake for one or both partners to find a substitute sexual partner; it is always damaging to the marriage. Extramarital affairs diminish the special quality of the marital relationship. This is true no matter how brief or superficial the affair, and even when there are extenuating circumstances. Sexual fidelity underlines and intensifies mutual consideration and intimacy; sexual infidelity always erodes it. When separation is necessary, the best thing is for the partners to view the deprivation as a joint stress that they must overcome together, rather than for one or both spouses to look for a substitute partner.

Consider, for instance, Sidney and Margaret. Sidney was in the military service and, when he transferred from the east to the west coast, she went with him. The move was very hard for her because she felt lonely and frightened and missed her family. She became pregnant, he was transferred overseas, and she returned home to her mother. The separation put tremendous pressure on her. She saw it as rejection, not something forced on her and her husband by the world. She felt unattractive, alone, and jealous, and worried about his being unfaithful to her. She eventually was able to get some professional help; her therapist offered emotional support through the difficult time of separation. Her husband also gave as much support as he could. He sent letters, made phone calls, sent little gifts and packages, and eventually, as soon as it was possible, arranged for her to join him. Both of them came to understand how hard it was for them to be separated and they resolved to minimize separation as much as they possibly could in the future.

The best methods for dealing with this problem are those that add to the happiness of each deprived partner without taking away from the marital relationship. If possible, find some way to make the separations shorter, or adjust both lives and careers to permit more time together. When separated, do things you like to do. Spend time with other adults in settings that minimize loneliness yet are not particularly seductive or sensual. Try to be with people with whom you have things in common but avoid situations which are beyond your threshold of sexual temptation.

Sometimes extramarital sexual activity seems to be a necessary choice even though it is far from ideal. Perhaps a couple can stand separation only by allowing each other the freedom to indulge in sexual activity with someone else. Such marriages have problems to begin with, because the partners are not capable of firm devotion to each other. Devotion means a willingness to undergo deprivation, to make a sacrifice for someone else. People who agree to extramarital sex during separation may be doing their very best, showing as much caring as they possibly can, but they are simply not champions of devotion. If they know themselves well enough, they usually realize that, when they have to be separated, they resent not being able to have sex with someone. They are afraid that, if lies become necessary, the marriage may not survive, so they decide to do the best they can, and one or both of them says "Go ahead."

It should be clearly understood that what may be necessary for this kind of marriage will harm a marriage of stronger people. Actually, even for weak marriages, extramarital sexual activity during separation is damaging. While it may enable the couple to stay together, the marriage will afterward be still weaker with less commitment. On the other hand, partners who have enough self-control, strength of character, and devotion to stay sexually faithful to each other despite the stress of being apart, will find the bond between them growing even stronger.

Differences in Appetite. There are some marriages in which the spouses' sexual appetites do not match. Nothing in this world is evenly divided, and spouses generally have different amounts of curiosity, desire, interest, and endurance. This becomes a problem when one of the partners is a sexual athlete and the other is sexually weaker.

Victor and Barbara, for instance, have this situation. They have been married eight years and have a three-year-old daughter. Victor owns a garage and works hard from early morning till late at night. His work is dirty and, when he comes home, he's tired. Also, by disposition, he's fastidious so he spends a lot of time cleaning himself after work. He also likes to play with their daughter and he helps Barbara around the house. For these reasons, although they are young, they're only able to have sex on weekends. Barbara is never as tired as Victor. She loves him and would be more than willing to have sex during the week. However, she understands and appreciates Victor and does not feel threatened. Although their sexual appetites are not the same, it's not a problem for them.

Jack and Frances, on the other hand, are in trouble. Frances needs a great deal of attention and reassurance and it's easy for her to feel rejected and bypassed. Jack has a physical job; he works hard and has many responsibilities. When he's tired and preoccupied with work, his interest in sex goes down.

This upsets Frances, who already feels insecure in their relationship, and she feels rejected. When Frances is tense and upset, she wants more closeness, more physical contact, and definitely more sex. Sex relaxes her; it makes her feel better, more alive, more successful, and more desirable. Frances has a strong sexual appetite while Jack has a much weaker one. Frances needs to be able to see that all of Jack's appetites are affected when he gets tired or preoccupied—eating and sleeping as well as sex. He should not be made to feel inadequate, or inferior, and most certainly not unmanly. Frances is fortunate to be so robust, but has to learn that it doesn't mean she's better than Jack. She must also become aware of her own stubbornness and anger when she cannot have what she wants.

Early in a marriage, sexually mismatched partners usually try hard to solve that dilemma. The weaker one tries to cover up his or her disinterest and is willing to have sex even when tired or not aroused. The athlete makes an effort to accept with grace the other's excuses; he or she realizes that the spouse is trying and believes there will be more and better sex later. As time goes on, it becomes harder for the weaker one to maintain his or her effort; the excuses tend to increase and each partner's tolerance for and acceptance of the other decreases.

This becomes a serious problem. Whether or not the marriage survives depends on the relationship's other strengths. If it has what the partner with the larger sexual appetite is looking for in other areas, if the partners feel that they mean much to one another, that they mean security to one another, and that the marriage is otherwise working or has worked well for them personally and socially, a couple will often be willing, indeed eager, to try to work out a mutually acceptable sexual arrangement with each other.

To do this, they need, first, to be sure that their sexual problem really is a matter of difference in appetite rather than personal rejection of one spouse by the other. Making certain there is no personal rejection is especially important for the person who wants more sex. And, emphatically, this person is as likely to be the woman as the man. Although men are said to have a greater desire for sex, that is not necessarily true, for many women have very large sexual appetites and many men have small ones. The point is that the one who does want more sex has to be able to feel sure that the other's lesser inclination is only a matter of desire and not a sign of rejection.

One way to evaluate this is to see if the partner with the smaller sex drive shows affection in other ways; does he/she freely give attention and tenderness? Keep in mind that individuals differ in how they show affection and how much affection they show. These differences are a matter of personality, and are directly related to the way a person was handled, fondled, and taken care of as a child.

In general, people with robust sexual appetites are physically affectionate, in large part because they received much warm physical affection from whoever took care of them when they were little. They are not afraid of affection; they like affection and where it can lead, so they do not hold back. They get right into touching, pressing, hugging, and kissing, and are delighted when it goes all the way. People with weak sexual appetites, on the other hand, are more likely to be physically cautious and withholding, generally because they were not handled and taken care of warmly as children. They tend to be afraid of the sex act so they don't want to start something that could lead to it. They are likely to show affection in other than physical ways. If they want to please, they bring gifts, they remember little things that the other person likes, they tend to be punctual, they remember phone calls, they send cards.

Another aspect of the fear of rejection is worry about the possibility that the partner may have an important sexual interest in someone outside the marriage. Naturally, people who are married are aware that there are other attractive people in the world, and indeed find some of them desirable or stimulating; such awareness, however, does not mean that a person is unhappy in his or her marriage or has sexual problems. To the contrary, it indicates that he or she is a healthy sexual being. There is a big difference between having feelings and doing something about them. But when sexual appetites differ, the mate with the larger sexual appetite is likely to become suspicious and alert, and to watch the spouse for any signs of desire for or even appreciation of the attractiveness of anyone else. Actually, for the partner with the smaller appetite to say that he or she finds someone else sexually attractive can be considered an encouraging sign of some sexual vitality, which is at least a step in the right direction. It is only when he or she suddenly somehow reveals a great affection for a person outside the marriage that suspicion is justified.

If the marriage is otherwise good; if there is clear affection on both sides; if no powerful extramarital attraction exists, then it is fair to assume that the sexual problem actually is one of different appetites, and the couple can at least try to learn how to cope with it. The one with the greater drive must moderate the issue, and at times tone down his or her sexual needs. Both partners need to try in various ways to increase the smaller appetite. Both partners must understand that different doesn't mean bad, but only different, and do what they can to help one another; only then will they be able to solve this particular problem. They may not ever achieve an ideal sexual relationship but at least they can work toward a solution to this problem.

The one with the greater sexual drive must not use himself or herself as a norm and preach to the other partner. Do not say, "I can make love anytime, anywhere, why can't you? I don't need cleanliness or quiet or the comfort of a bed or background music or half an hour to get into the mood, you shouldn't either." If the spouse requires certain special conditions in order to respond, then everything possible should be done to fulfill them.

The more active sexual partner must listen closely to what the other says: "This afternoon would have been fine, when I was less tired"; "It's better when your body's nice and clean"; "Not when the children are running through the house, and not when the in-laws are visiting." Then he or she needs to act on what is said. Any effort to be supportive will be well compensated by the return in sexual responsiveness from the frailer sexual partner, who is exposing himself or herself, perhaps quite bravely, by confiding what is sexually arousing. The spouse needs to realize this, get the message, and accommodate it, rather than think or even worse, say, "Oh, that's silly, you don't need all that. It shouldn't be like that. I don't need that."

It will also be helpful if the stronger sexual partner tries to be more observant and more attuned to the other partner, and tries to devise ways to arouse him or her. Does the partner need more foreplay? More leisurely intercourse? More attention afterward? What will help to stimulate and sustain the sexual appetite—what's the right setting, or the right garments, flowers, food? What is most evocative for this particular person?

Anything that can be done to increase the feelings of self-worth of the one with the weaker appetite is good. People who are not easily aroused sexually may require additional foreplay to get excited, including foreplay that is not directly sexual, that takes place perhaps quite a while before the two people go to bed. Such people often need a great deal of attention, affection, companionship—their mates should listen to them, walk with them, talk with them, do with them the things they like to do. This kind of attention warms them, makes them feel more worthwhile, and more able to give, sexually as well as in other ways. Finally, sometimes life itself will warm them. We all have times when we feel particularly good about ourselves, periods of relaxation instead of work, periods of personal happiness. During such good times, they too may be able to have a more fulfilling sex life with far less preparation and care.

At some times, though, the one with the sturdier appetite will have to find other outlets for his or her sexual energy—involvement with the children, work, or sports, doing things around the house, whatever. Certainly it is less than ideal to substitute one outlet for another. If you're thirsty, you should drink. It's very hard to quench your thirst by eating food, even though there's fluid in food. The best way to quench the sexual appetite is by having sex. But if it's not always possible, then sexual energy can be diverted to other things. It smooths life out if the sexually sturdier person is able to do this with good grace. It is most important to try to avoid reacting to the smaller appetite as a rejection maneuver.

The one with the weaker appetite has to accept the fact that he or she is not a sexual athlete. In our culture, that's a painful admission, because we admire athletes and champions, including sexual athletes and champions. It is possible to keep the fact that you are not a sexual athlete a secret from other people; but you should never keep it a secret from yourself and it will be helpful if you can let your spouse in on your secret. Self-deception here can lead to disaster. A person who does not start off with much sexual strength needs to come to terms with his or her deficit. But you can't start to do this until you acknowledge that it's true.

The sexually weaker person who does not admit the truth to himself or herself is likely to reproach the partner for being oversexed or unreasonable—silently, if not out loud. But just as the stronger partner needs to understand and be accepting, so does the weaker one. It's unkind to try to protect yourself from the realization that you do not have a strong sex drive by berating a spouse who does. Even if you experience the partner as greedy and demanding, it is better to understand and respect differences—and try to adjust to them. Ask yourself: "What can I do to improve my appetite for sex? Can it be raised in some way, stretched, made better?" Self-knowledge is the key.

If you're tired—from working, partying, drinking, sports, charitable activities, taking care of the children, whatever—does your ability to function sexually decrease or even disappear? If so, you should remember that sex is an important, indeed a necessary element of a gratifying marriage and stop doing some of whatever it is that is wearing you out. You may have to work less, even though this costs money; you may have to spend less time on child care, even if the children might not like it. Put less energy into gardening, golf, fishing, keeping house, baking, drinking with the boys, talking with the girls. Learn to allot your energy and save some of it for vital activities. If being happily married is one of your priorities, leave enough time and energy to be able to have some gratifying sex.

Avoidance and Affairs. An adequate sex life is one of the legitimate expectations from marriage and, in all cultures, it is considered a serious breach of the marital contract when one partner deprives the other of sex. Even cultures that do not recognize divorce consider a marriage in which there is no consistent sexual activity a marriage that is not valid and will allow its annulment. Sexual deprivation is indeed a very legitimate cause for annulment or divorce.

Sexual desire varies throughout adult life, with periods of greater and lesser intensity, so that sexual activity is both more frequent and more enjoyable at some times than it is at others. This is one strong reason why marital partners need tolerance and sympathy for one another. Over many years of marriage their sexual relationship will change, and it is to be expected that at certain times one or the other partner will not be at a sexual peak. There are even times when one or the other partner in a marriage may turn away from sex entirely or almost entirely. Such temporary avoidance of sex occurs in many marriages.

Such a period has to be stressful, but avoidance does not necessarily signify a loss of love or affection. The partner who avoids sex may be too drained by some other stress to have much interest in or energy for it. Real external stress—work, study, a new baby, moving—may diminish the sexual appetite. So can a psychological upheaval, like a depression the causes of which may not be apparent to somebody else, or a depression caused by external stress such as excessive work, or too many children, or failure at work or at school. If the marriage is essentially sound, and a spouse starts to avoid sex for such a reason, the other spouse should be accepting and supportive. The marriage can ordinarily survive if the partners join their resources to overcome whatever is causing the trouble—including getting professional help if it seems necesary.

It is more serious when one partner turns away sexually because he or she feels angry or hurt or disappointed with the other and therefore feels less love and desire. Then the other partner is likely to feel hurt, deprived, belittled, or rejected. If it is a matter of a recent misunderstanding, usually it can be worked through, provided it is attacked vigorously before it becomes chronic and therefore malignant and leads to other bad consequences. In cases like this, psychiatric intervention can be very helpful and should be encouraged, because it will help clarify the cause for the avoidance of sex. It may be something as trivial as retaliation for an insult. Insight into the problem can soothe and reassure, so that the incident is merely a temporary experience.

It is a much more serious thing when one partner no longer loves or desires or esteems or even likes the other. This may result from something one partner did that the other cannot forgive, or from the way life turns out, the way two people change over the years, or perhaps experiences that they cannot handle together in a mutually sustaining and supporting way. People with this kind of problem may seek the help of a psychiatrist, especially when one of the partners avoids sex and the other partner still wants it and feels hurt and disappointed, annoyed and cheated. Sometimes matters can be resolved, and the marriage becomes sexually workable again. Sometimes damage is so deep that not even the most skillfull intervention can turn things around, and either the marriage is ripped apart or the partners continue to live together unhappily.

Some marriages have little sexual activity, because neither of the partners any longer feels much sexual attraction toward the other. Somehow there has been a mutual dulling of desire. Since marriage fulfills needs besides sex, many people will choose to stay married even when there is little sexual desire between them, so that both of them want little sexual activity. A relaxed, easy-going life situation? Far from it. These marriages may endure for years and may be successful in some other areas, but there is no avoiding the fact that both partners will be under stress. If they have any spark of sexual feeling for each other, there is no way they can live together without having sex and not feel stressed. The partners can stay together, learn to tolerate the situation, continue the marriage for reasons other than sex, and make it a stable marriage; but it will be a wounded marriage.

Some people in marriages where the sex isn't working right will acknowledge their problem individually or even to one another and still continue the marriage. This openness is conducive to mental health. People who don't acknowledge the truth are prone to psychological and psychosomatic symptoms. Some get migraine headaches; some develop a fear of flying. Many people who cannot bear to admit to themselves that they are in a sexually miserable marriage may try to hide from the truth by becoming very busy—in their community, their church, their firehouse, their ambulance corps, their house. They may use alcohol to keep fooling themselves by dulling their senses and mind so the problem of sexual dissatisfaction in the marriage is less obvious to them; unfortunately it becomes more complicated and difficult to handle. A person who is drunk is even less able to perform sexually.

Sex is not an issue if married people do not care for one another at all. If husband and wife have turned away from one another and no longer experience any desire for one another, they may continue to live together and never approach each other sexually. They may, depending on their personal circumstances, decide to stay together out of fear, financial need, social pressures, church pressures, their children's needs, their age, their personal problems, their health. If they are old, tired, and defeated, they may simply give up on sex, and continue to live together as two asexual beings.

If they are more vigorous and alive than that and yet choose to stay together for their own reasons, they may work out an arrangement whereby they each have their own sexual outlets outside the marriage—that is, they will turn to extramarital sex. If they are reluctant to break up their marriage, they may agree to tolerate extramarital sexual activities by one or both of them. (It says much for the institution of marriage that even when the sexual situation is unsatisfactory, and the partners feel they have to go outside the marriage to seek sexual fulfillment, they still often find the marriage itself worthwhile.)

Extramarital arrangements may be openly discussed and deliberately agreed upon; an affair may be viewed as an adventure, or as something to satisfy curiosity. It is much more common, however, for one or both of the partners to get secretly involved in sexual activity outside the marriage. Often the sexual encounters simply happen—one of the frustrated partners meets someone at work, in the neighborhood, at some social function, through an organization—and a sexual alliance develops. Some such affairs are very short; others last a long time.

An affair, acknowledged or secret, involving one or both partners, may be experienced as very fulfilling by the people involved but, in relation to the marriage, it is a mistake. When it is over, the people in the marriage have to cope somehow with the fact that it happened. They must learn how to go on in spite of it, to recover from it. If it was a clandestine affair, the offended partner needs to forgive, if possible; the other partner must try to win forgiveness or at least acceptance. Marriages can recover from extramarital affairs, but under no circumstances do extramarital sexual activities improve or enrich the marriage.

Some people will argue that an affair does improve marriage. At the moment when the affair is at its peak, they are happy, exhilarated, excited, occupied with the affair, and paying less attention to the marriage, so the marriage seems to be better; it is not. They may be more cheerful and less cranky, grouchy, and difficult to live with, but the affair, at the same time, is taking time, energy, money, and love away from the marriage. It diminishes exactly those activities that are the important purposes of marriage—companionship, recreation, financial resources meant for the family, time for the children, and all the love and tenderness that belong in the marriage. If the affair is secret, there are the additional problems of hiding, cheating, and making up credible alibis. If the affair is in the open, it amounts to a public admission of the marriage's failure, a confession that one of them has had to go outside the marriage to find a special sexual relationship.

If both partners have affairs, it is harder on a marriage and more likely that the marriage will break up. Marriage is a partnership and, if one of the partners wants to keep it going, it's more likely to hold together, for a while at least. If only one is having an affair, at least the other one, for whatever reason, is not—perhaps because he or she still loves and is sexually attracted to the other and is therefore willing to be loyal and dedicated. There may be less healthy reasons, however. The faithful one may be too afraid or too dependent, may lack the necessary self-confidence and self-esteem to try to find new happiness outside the marriage. But even these unhealthy reasons may be powerful enough to keep the marriage together.

If both partners are having affairs, obviously both are dissatisfied. If both keep their affairs secret, however, they still may be hoping that the marriage will improve; at least each wants to minimize the risk that it will get weaker and possibly break up. They are sticking it out. If both are having open affairs, they are openly flaunting the failure of the marriage, and there is very little hope that the marriage will survive.

Consider what happened to Ron and Lucy, for example. Both were professionals who wore fashionable clothes and did all the "in" things. They were both aware that they were dissatisfied with their marriage and tried what they considered to be appropriately intellectualized solutions, including applied management techniques. If something is missing in your life, you identify what is missing and add it. Both decided that what they were missing was sexual excitement so, first one and then the other started to have affairs.

When they still had hope for their marriage, they kept their affairs secret; but, of course, their extramarital arrangements did not add any magic to their marriage. Their real problem was that they had selected each other for very superficial reasons—their mutual interest in being with the right people, wearing the right clothes, visiting the right places, doing the right things. They never reached a level of genuine intimacy and their sex life, which was the area on which they focused, was superficial and inadequate. Having affairs outside the marriage was no solution, because it had nothing to do with their real problem, which was learning to understand their real needs so that they could address themselves to filling those needs in appropriate ways.

When their secret affairs did not help, each decided they were not yet free enough sexually, and they started to tell each other about their affairs. That didn't help either. They decided that they should try more elaborate and modern sexual solutions outside the marriage, rather like taking an expensive vacation when a cheap one turned out to be boring. They found another couple and began an open sexual relationship with them. The intensity of feeling was not the same for all four participants. The pleasure received was not the same for all, and the sexual thrills were not equally distributed. The shifts of emotional commitment and loyalty were great, and only increased the emotional strains. Now Ron and Lucy are divorced.

Some couples say, after one of them has had an affair, or both have, that they have become closer. If they are closer, it's because they have successfully withstood the stress together, not because their extramarital activity itself in any way improved their relationship. People who say they have a better marriage after they've had one or a couple of affairs are often trying to avoid the consequences of their behavior. It helps relieve their feelings of guilt. If they suggest they've done something helpful for their marriage, they think people will be less critical of them. Even if they do now have a better, more stable marriage, it is, again, better because it has survived a stress. The bond between them has been revived, and they have renewed their commitment through surviving the hurt, even though some of them may not understand this yet.

It's difficult for spouses to live together and not have good sex if there is any spark of mutual attraction between them, but it's even harder if there is a one-sided attraction. Terrible feelings of frustration, deprivation, anger, and hurt arise in this situation; a tendency to retaliate emerges, a wish to hurt in retaliation.

Sexual avoidance is a very common cause of divorce. It should be, because, after all, sex is one of the very basic reasons for getting married. Sometimes it indicates deep-seated psychosexual problems in the partner who is avoiding sex. There may be a problem of impotence or frigidity that this person covers up by avoiding sex, a problem due to some deep personal hurt whose occurrence is lost to memory.

Such a hurt may be the result of some dreadful and extraordinary childhood experience—physical abuse from a loved parent, being badly frightened by having to witness indiscreet parents behave immodestly, perhaps sexual molestation up to and including rape. Such encounters perhaps wouldn't damage some children, but they do have extraordinary effects on others. For instance, one little girl was molested by her stepfather, whom she also saw being cruel to her mother. Or, to take another case, a neighbor seduced a little boy who was very lonely and starved for affection. He therefore in some way passively participated in the seduction, which later made him feel extremely guilty. The girl grows up frigid, and has trouble relating to men at all. The boy becomes a man who isn't aware of his guilt anymore, but is almost always impotent.

Of course, everyone's sexual ability and sexual potency vary with mood, the desirability of a sexual partner, the degree of self-esteem, and many other factors. That is a very different matter from the extraordinary conditions we are talking about here, which may be called "psychosexual illnesses." Fortunately they are somewhat rare, and people who do suffer from them certainly should seek psychiatric help.

A person may avoid sex in marriage because he or she is a homosexual. Such people may deny to themselves the fact that they are homosexual and try to hide from it. If it seems difficult or at least personally inconvenient to be homosexual, they will keep this central fact about themselves pretty much out of their own awareness. Or, if they are aware, they may cover up their lesbian or male homosexual orientation. They are so interested in the social or other advantages of marriage that they go ahead and marry in the hope that they can bluff their way through. Realistically, they cannot. Obviously, there is a problem if a homosexual is married to a heterosexual. At the most basic level, a homosexual wants to be and live like a homosexual and therefore does not want to be living with a heterosexual. The homosexual person is pretending to be what he or she is not.

Take Mabel, for example—a handsome woman of forty-four, bright and capable, with a good job. Her boss is a very successful businessman who relies upon her. She is a wonderful assistant, loyal, hard-working, glad to serve him and share in his exciting life. Mable has been married twelve years. She seeks psychiatric treatment from time to time, each time with a different therapist, to deal with crises that arise in her marriage. She is "a wonderful patient"—she keeps appointments and pays her bills promptly, but she doesn't stay in therapy. She comes for two or three visits, thanks the therapist profusely, seems grateful for the help, but is never able or willing to let the therapy progress past the point of the immediate crisis.

Her husband Roy is a handsome man of forty-nine, an executive. Roy is a homosexual. They met at work when she was thirty-two, and became friends. Roy told her that he'd been gay, but assured her that he had changed and had it under control. Mabel's decision to marry Roy reflected her character. She does not have great expectations for herself, does not have a very high degree of self-esteem. She decided that, as long as she had a companion, somebody to talk to, somebody to share her problems with, somebody to go out with, she could be "happy"; in a word, she thought that marrying Roy was the best that she could do. She found him physically attractive, she was impressed with his intelligence, she enjoyed their time together, and she thought that living with him was something she would be able to handle.

Mabel was the oldest of seven children and helped her mother raise the other children. She assumed a great deal of family responsibility, and went without a college education so that she could work to help support the family. She gets pleasure from doing the right thing and being helpful and, as a child, she always felt that her goodness was the only special thing she had. She entered adulthood without great expectations. She enjoyed work, and always related to the men in her office as a colleague rather than as an attractive or flirtatious woman. When Roy asked her to marry him at age thirty-two, she therefore thought it was a great opportunity. She's paid a heavy price. She regrets not having had children. Roy has tried hard to be a good husband, but through their twelve years together, his passions have gotten the best of him many times. He then does impulsive things, spends a lot of money, neglects Mabel, and acts irresponsibly at his job. Mabel always feels threatened by the possibility of abandonment and rejection. She stays in the marriage because it's too much of a risk to do anything else, and she goes for help whenever her burden grows especially heavy. Roy is sorry, but he can't help it. He keeps falling in love.

Marriages between a heterosexual and a homosexual can last, although both people are likely to be terribly unhappy. Nor is it always the homosexual who works to continue the marriage. Some heterosexuals are so terrified to be alone that they will put up with bizarre and sometimes even dangerous arrangements with their spouses so as not to break up a marriage. Strangers will be brought into the house, or the homosexual husband or wife is forever sneaking out to find illicit lovers, sometimes even giving them money that is needed for the family. The drive toward sexual fulfillment is very powerful. Their spouses often don't know with whom or where they are.

There is something terribly sad about a heterosexual who is willing to stay in this kind of marriage. Usually he or she has an extremely poor self-image, great insecurity, and great dependency needs. Such people may be quite successful, have good jobs, be the functioning, smart, capable, providing partners in the marriage, but be afraid that if they lose this partner they will never find another one. They tend to think that they are very undeserving and unworthwhile human beings.

I am very much against this kind of energy-draining liaison. Partners in this kind of marriage should seek professional help and explore the option of dissolving their difficult union. Marriage is conducive to a heterosexual life, and people who are seeking homosexual or bisexual activity will find conventional marriage very unsatisfactory.

Obsessive Sex. Sometimes when one partner complains that the other demands too much sex, the complaining partner is trying to avoid sex, and considers even normal sexual demands excessive. On the other hand, the complaint may be realistic. Sex can become an obsession—the desires of one partner seem to be insatiable, there is marathon sex, there are frequent or constant demands for new varieties, new positions, new settings, new clothing, new scents, new lighting, new everything. Under these circumstances, sex is probably being used by one of the partners for reasons other than sexual fulfillment.

A sexual arrangement is satisfactory when the sexual activities—elaborate or not—are enjoyed by both partners. A couple should be able to relax together, be open together, have sex for a longer time than just the mimimum required for intercourse, be free enough with one another to experience intense closeness and explore sexually, try different positions, try sex in different settings and at different times. It can be playful to try to enrich the experience by use of clothing, scents, food, and drink. And if both people want to spend a lot of time doing any or all these things, or just plain having sex, why not? There is no such thing as too much sex. The amount of time and energy available to the human organism is limited, of course. If a great deal is spent in sexual activity, there will be less time and energy for other things. The physiological limits on sexual performance are firmer than those on, say, eating and drinking, so if you try to have more sex than you're physiologically capable of, the body will simply not perform. But otherwise, if that's the relaxation and recreation the partners choose, it will neither damage them nor the marriage.

The partners don't have to have exactly the same intensity of desire or like all positions and activities equally well, but sex should be experienced as pleasurable by both. When one partner wants to try new varieties of sex that the other partner always thwarts, it will become a source of friction. So will any tendency of one partner to interpret a healthy appetite for sex in the other as an attempt to use sex for some camouflaged internal purpose. On the other hand, when one partner has to indulge in sex many times a week and is always looking for new activities, and still has a lingering sense of dissatisfaction and no interest in how the other partner feels, sex is probably being used for something other than sex.

What may be considered the normal and right amount of sex varies tremendously from couple to couple, and for the same couple under different circumstances. Are they on vacation? Are they getting ready for some hectic time like Christmas, remodeling their house, working overtime because it is the season in his or her business? Any of these circumstances can change their amount of sex in one direction or the other. But, in general, when a couple is having sex daily or twice or three times daily, unless they are on their honeymoon, or they've been apart for some time, or they're on vacation, or some other very exceptional circumstance exists, they are having sex with unusually high frequency. If they are both happy and they can handle it, then indeed they are very fortunate, and may consider themselves sexual champions, because this is more sex than most people can handle for any extended period of time. Usually however, this frequency means that someone is using sex to try to satisfy other than sexual needs, and thus is using his or her partner in an unhealthy way.

It is quite common for sexual appetite and sexual activity to decrease under conditions of tension, anxiety, or depression, but some people indulge in a lot of sex during times of such inner stress to satisfy other than sexual needs. Thus, one or the other partner in a marriage may demand sexual activity as a tranquilizer, to make it possible to go to sleep, as an antidote for depression, to allay anxiety in the morning and make it seem bearable to get up and go to work. Sometimes, if it's possible, sex is demanded again during the day. Using sex like this means that one partner is not facing whatever problems are at the root of the anxiety or other misery. It is extremely draining on the other partner. It takes the pleasure and fulfillment out of sex. Sexual problems are very likely to develop. The partner who is being used begins to feel like a sexual object, which leads to anger and resentment. The result often is a turning away from sex, an unwillingness or even inability to participate in sex. Or, the used partner may feel inadequate because he or she is not able to live up to all the sexual demands.

Coming together in sexual activity during times of inner stress can be very reassuring, loving, and helpful. Here sex is used not as an escape mechanism, but as an expression of mutual devotion, support, and loyalty. But other steps must also be taken at the same time to understand and solve the problems of the stressed partner. The couple needs to confront the difficulty together, discuss it openly, and try to find a solution. Their support for one another is thus expressed in sex, which is a very healthy way of using it, as opposed to demanding more sex without explaining honestly that he or she needs it because of, say, anxiety or depression.

Even here, though, if there is love between the partners, the problem can be handled. The first thing is to give support and reassurance and go along with the other person's sexual demands. It is usually fairly easy to do when the excessive sexual demands are made only during a particularly critical time. It becomes much more difficult to be giving when, as sometimes happens, the sex escalates into a continuous tension-release mechanism, and the abused partner grows more and more tired, angry, and resentful. It is very good to express these feelings, to try to talk about them to the partner before the anger and resentment build into a volcano that erupts all over the partner. This "before it's too late" talk may sometimes get through to the demanding partner and enable him or her to see more of what is really going on. When it doesn't, professional help may be extremely useful for establishing norms and understanding motivations.

Some individuals who are disappointed or frustrated by life may try to use their sexual ability to reassure themselves. There is, of course, nothing wrong and everything right with coming together with one's spouse and expressing love and admiration sexually at a time of adversity. Nor is there anything wrong if one of the elements of lovemaking is gaining reassurance from being able to make love strongly and confidently at such a time. It is a completely different situation when a person who is frustrated by, say, a failure at work, comes home and acts like the ruler of the world by performing insatiable sexual feats not *with* the partner, but *on* the partner. The difference, of course, lies in the performer's relation to the partner, who, with good reason, is likely to experience this sexual activity as personally insulting.

Unfortunately, these people are suffering from feelings of low esteem. They can't open up, admit their weakness, and ask for support honestly, but rather begin to bicker with their mates and generally put them down. In some cases they use sex to do that, demanding and engaging in it in an arrogant, belittling, and therefore degrading manner.

Herbert is one man who uses sex to reinforce his self-esteem. He's a handsome man, well built, although not very tall, the oldest of three, the only boy. His father had great hopes for him, but Herbert was not much of a scholar and did not do well in school, and though he was a good athlete, his small size kept him back. He was, however, very popular with girls, and even as an adolescent he used that fact to cover up frustrations, disappointments, and lack of achievement.

Herbert is married to Myrna; he has a job that is steady and stable, but not exciting or adventurous, with a great deal of routine. Herbert has had some success at work, but in between each promotion there's been a long interval of frustration. Myrna loves and accepts him, but he's terribly jealous of her and not always particularly attentive to her needs. Whenever they go out, no matter what the occasion, he becomes horrendously jealous if she talks to any other man. On the other hand, he talks to all the other women, and flirts and jokes. His sexual performance is somewhat spotty. He likes sex, and he's always interested in it; he has periods of great sexual need, when he wants sex frequently, daily, twice daily. He wants oral sex, anal sex. He wants sex while watching television. Myrna likes sex; she's sexually uninhibited, but during these episodes there is no pleasing him. No amount of sex is enough. No amount of experimentation or variety, positions or props satisfies him. At these times, she is cool to him. He calls her frigid, inhibited, unattractive, too fat, not built right. These episodes of sexual frenzy and dissatisfaction, and even sexual cruelty, occur when he has difficulty with his job, when he has been bypassed for a promotion, when in some way he feels he is not appreciated as a human being, as a person, or as a man.

Linda also uses sex as a weapon, although in the opposite way. Linda's parents had a stormy marriage and, as a child, Linda always took her mother's side. She felt that her father took advantage of his wife's dependent position as a homemaker and a mother and treated her poorly, because, as a man, he felt he was superior. Furthermore, Linda believed that her father favored his sons, and was much more understanding and lenient with them than he was with Linda and her sister. Linda is a professional in a health-related field, married to a professional man her own age. They have agreed to share responsibilities—they both go to work and they both take care of the house. Linda feels that her husband does not live up to their agreement; she says he frequently takes unfair advantage of her, that he does only the jobs that he likes to do, and leaves her to do all the chores that must be done whether she likes to do them or not.

Linda likes sex and feels that both partners ought to initiate it. Before they were married, Linda and her husband had an excellent sex life. They were free and loving and warm. They liked vigorous foreplay and both felt satisfied. Since they have been married, however, their sex life has deteriorated. It is harder and harder to please Linda. She demands more and more foreplay and, if things don't go exactly her way, she will say, at even a most passionate moment, "I'm not in the mood anymore," and will call it quits.

In general, Linda is not happy in the marriage. She feels that her needs for understanding, attention, and support are not being met, that she is not appreciated, and that she's getting the short end of the stick. She's completely unaware that she is using sex to punish her husband because she is unhappy in her marriage. She's using it to make him feel inadequate and to frustrate him sexually. Whenever she's angry with him, she says "I'm not ready, you're just using me," and cuts the activity short or even simply ends it by getting out of bed.

The wounds that people try to heal through sexual activity are many and varied. It depends on what is important to them, what activities usually give them good feelings about themselves, what they base their identity on. Men or women for whom business success is a key value will respond very poorly to failure in business, and may try to make up for it through great success in bed. People who are not satisfied with their athletic abilities may try to compensate similarly: "I may not be much on the tennis courts, but I'm a champion in bed." People who have problems with fertility may be tempted to compensate for that with lots of sexual activity. People may use sex to ease the pain of growing older.

Once again, there is nothing wrong in using whatever you have, whatever you enjoy, whatever you're good at to get more out of life and feel better about yourself. Sex can be useful for this, and couples who can reassure one another by their honest admiration and sexual desire for one another are lucky. There is a problem, though, when one spouse uses sex to boost himself or herself while at the same time, because of feelings of inadequacy, uses sex to put the other spouse down. Sex used in this way becomes a serious stress on a marriage, and requires professional help.

VARIETIES OF MARITAL SEX

Sexual Preference. Sexual preferences are a matter of personal taste and style, not absolutes. No one particular preference makes people either superior or inferior, inadequate, degraded, or perverted. Ideally, a couple's activity will be entirely acceptable, desirable, and enjoyable to both. Short of that ideal sitation, a couple can enjoy their sex more if they learn to cooperate with each other's tastes. They will stand a better chance of doing this if they view sexual preferences as a matter of taste, not a matter of power, talent, or judgment, and avoid using preferences to separate the good guys from the bad. If the couple cannot or will not work out a sexual arrangement that is acceptable to both of them, their marriage will be stressed. It will be more stressed if, in addition, either partner degrades the other's sexual preferences as inferior, unimaginative or bizarre, indecent, overathletic, not sexy, or whatever.

Our sexual preferences and desires are influenced by how we were taken care of in earliest childhood, how we were washed, nursed, changed, cuddled, played with, toilet trained, chastised, whether we were spanked or not. Children of young and vigorous parents who laugh with them and toss them up in the air are more apt to grow up to like horseplay in bed than children whose parents hardly ever treated them freely and warmly. That's why people who on the surface appear quite similar have such diverse sexual tastes and desires. Attributes such as intellect, ideals, drive, profession, and prosperity do not predict what a person's sexual preferences will be. And to complicate things further, people do not always and under all circumstances have the same sexual desires. On a very simple level, for instance, sometimes they may want to have the light on, sometimes not. Or they may go through a period of liking oral sex, then no longer desire it. All this adds up to a situation where the chance for great gratification stands right next to the chance for great frustration.

The Advantages of Marital Sex. Most people desire, expect, and demand frequent sexual activity, and it is one of the things marriage offers. A good stable marriage also allows the spouses an opportunity to express themselves sexually and to experiment sexually—to try different positions, different movements, different settings so that they can develop their sexual style and find out more about themselves, find out what kind of sexual activities are most conducive to their happiness.

Once both partners are sure that they will have sex regularly and frequently, they can do some experimenting. For instance, do they prefer sex in the evening, in the morning, in the middle of the night, during the week, on weekends? And where do they want to have sex? Most sexual activity takes place in bed, because it's convenient, but people can just as easily make love on a carpet in the living room. Sex out of doors becomes complicated, but if the weather conditions are right, the spot comfortable, the privacy secure, and if the fancies of both partners are moved by the setting, why not?

It is not a good idea for children to observe adults in sexual intercourse, indoors or out. When little children see two adults climbing on one another and hear them making the kinds of sounds people make during sexual activity, two things happen. One is that the children themselves become stimulated, often tremendously so, but do not understand the stimulation and don't know what to do with it. They are thus confused and overwhelmed by emotion over which they have no control. The second is that children usually are frightened by seeing the sex act. They perceive it as violent, and become terrified at the spectacle of father hurting mother.

These reactions may or may not in themselves be dangerous to children, but how they are handled is crucial. The best thing to do is for the adults to end the sex act as soon as they can and then treat the child who has entered the room very gently and warmly. Sometimes, however, one parent will withdraw and the other will either hit or berate the child: "You're four years old, why can't you stay put? Go right back to bed this instant." The child obeys, but is still terrified. The end result, especially if the aggressive parent is often unkind or difficult, may be a serious sexual impairment in adulthood.

Changes. A couple can make their sex life much more interesting and colorful by changing time and place and atmosphere. "Let's make love by the fireplace, and let's have the music on." "Let's leave the blinds open so we can see the sun and hear the wind." "Let's have the blinds drawn so it's dark and cozy." "Let's leave the light on so we can watch what we're doing and look at one another and see everything."

A consistent preference for any such style can become a problem if the partners don't share it, so that they fight about it. The statement "My way is right" usually comes out sounding like a general principle. One partner wants the light on, and the other insists that "only whores do it when it's light." Or one may say, "I'm willing to have sex on the beach, in the woods, on the carpet, anywhere, but you won't touch me unless we're in bed. You have no imagination, no flair—you're practically atrophied." It takes only one to start such a fight, but both partners have to suffer in it. The problem lies not in the time or place or the variety, but is the inability or unwillingness to understand that differences make life more interesting, that a couple's differences can supplement and complement each other. This problem is compounded, in some cases, by a desire to insult or make fun of a sexual partner.

As far as the timing of sexual activity is concerned, people tend to feel sexy or not for their own physiological or psychological reasons. Some feel more interested in sex when they are rested and relaxed, others when they are tense, since they enjoy sex because it is a release. Arguments about this have less to do with when they should have sex, and more to do with the relationship, especially if one of the pair keeps insisting that "my way is better," instead of trying to see how they can work things out together.

Like all of adult life, sex requires foresight, planning, and a measure of self-discipline. That's why potions and aphrodisiacs are so alluring—they claim to make foresight unnecessary and any sexual contact immediately successful. In *Midsummer Night's Dream* Shakespeare wrote about sprinkling a person's eyelids with magic drops that make the next person seen instantly lovable and desirable. Even in the twentieth century and four-fifths of the way to the twenty-first, people still dream about a magic way to make all men and women desirable and responsive and tender. That's why so many businesses catering to this fantasy are successful. From furniture to music, from clothing to cosmetics, everything is touted as helping to make a couple more relaxed and sensually inclined.

But no vitamin will make all people into powerful and ardent lovers, and neither will wheat germ, olives, mangoes, rare steak, or caviar. If a man and woman who are attracted to each other eat exotic and very good food together in a secluded place at a time when they are free to have sex, they are very likely to experience two pleasant sensual activities, good food and good sex, and two good things are better than one. But actually the sexual electricity between them is more likely to make the eating pleasurable than the eating is to make them feel sexy. And if two people who do not find each other sexually exciting eat food together, no matter how exquisite or exotic, it won't improve their chances of moving on to a good sexual experience with each other.

The same applies to other substances or objects used to improve the quality of love. Some of them have aphrodisiac qualities for some people under some conditions. At times people who are functioning well and have healthy sexual appetities find fantasy-provoking power in lace, perfume, leather, silk, satin, a soft voluptuous bed, a hard puritan bed, a water bed, white sheets, black sheets, floral sheets, mirrors in the room. Why not? It's fun. But whatever substance or object a person prefers, its power, its magic, its ability to "turn me on" is lodged in the psyche, in the fantasies of the person. For some people, a particular material or smell or object may be so important as to serve as an enabler—to make them psychologically and physiologically able to have sex—but that is still a specific personal psychological preference.

Sexual play like this becomes a problem when one partner is somehow turned off by the other's fantasies—when the fantasies of one, instead of being seen by the other as playful, seductive, or fun, are seen as sadistic, degrading, or perverted, or in some other way having a very unpleasant connotation. This negative reaction may be unfortunate. For instance, a man who feels more powerful and vigorous if he wears a seductive pair of leather shorts and even likes sometimes to dress up as a Roman soldier is not necessarily a sadist or a homosexual. A woman who wants to wear a flamboyant and transparent dressing gown which she throws aside to reveal very lacy red underwear is just doing that. It is possible, indeed likely, that both of these people are offering themselves more completely as sexual partners, sharing their innermost fantasies, as an expression of love and trust—a sign that they feel secure and safe enough for profound self-exposure. If one partner is sadistic or homosexual or disloyal, it is much more likely to become apparent in other ways.

Talking during sexual activity can be stimulating. Not enough is said about the sensuality of talk. We can conjure up strong pictures and create beautiful fantasies, and reassure one another with words. It can be a great stimulant to say to another person, "I love you and I want you"; indeed such words, when backed up by feelings, by truth, are probably the most powerful aphrodisiac of all.

Ordinary soap and water can also help to make sexual partners more appealing to each other. Many people overlook the courtesy of a clean body. A great deal of sexual discord can arise over poor personal hygiene—the husband's or the wife's dirty underarms, feet, hair, teeth and consequently breath, and sexual organs. Most of us do not have perfect figures, magnificent loins, fabulous bosoms or chests. Most of us carry signs and scars of illness and aging. Nonetheless, we can all clean ourselves regularly. It's true that some people do get aroused by the smell of sweaty, dirty bodies, though not many. Each person does have a personally distinctive body odor, which may be partly attractive to sexual partners; still, enough of this odor comes through even after bathing.

The fact is that much pain and misery are expressed in psychiatric consultations about one partner's simply refusing to wash. He or she sees the partner's requests for cleanliness as a sign of lack of love and attraction, and also as an attempt to gain control. Washing and cleaning the body have symbolic meanings for many people. The reason is that as infants we were changed, cleansed, and washed by other people. These intimate acts take on sensual overtones, because it is at these times that infants are most often held, handled, and fondled. The sensual overtones stay with us into adulthood, so that the area of personal hygiene always has some degree of symbolic importance. People who won't wash are likely to have experienced their early cleansing not as tender, but as restrictive or rough manipulation that they were powerless to prevent. There is no simple scenario for how this is apt to affect them, but almost always they lose awareness of those early days, and usually just think of themselves as relaxed and carefree about cleanliness.

It might seem that it would be easy to get a husband or wife to change in this regard, but actually it's very difficult.

The couple has to talk about it and negotiate the issue. Usually it is wise not to attack the offender head on, but rather to say something like, "You've done other things for me, could you put up with this cleanliness thing of mine?" In fact, this is in general a good way to approach a mate over disagreements. Even on such a relatively simple issue as whether someone is clean or not, it is possible to overreact.

Many couples find some festive activity—an evening at the theater, a dance, a picnic—a fine way to set the right mood for love. Sex is then like a liqueur after a very good dinner. Sometimes, of course, you're satisfied by the food and wine and dessert and would rather not have the liqueur. If a couple has been out on the town, after a hectic day of working in the yard and taking care of the kids, one partner may not want sex or may not have the energy for it. But the other partner may insist, having the firm idea that sex at this point is an essential part of the good life, and making love is the thing to do as the grand finale of a big day and evening. If the partner refuses or simply can't, the other one may take it as a personal rejection or an affront. Rigid ideas about how things ought to be are at fault here, but there is more to the problem than this. For good sex after a big evening, as for many other things in marriage, there is no substitute for caring and good judgment along the way.

Foreplay. To define foreplay as touching and fondling right before the act of intercourse is to take too narrow a view. In a sense foreplay includes all the signs that male and female send one another acknowledging awareness of the other's sexuality, and indicating interest and desire. Understood this way, it can include the way they say hello and goodbye, or the way they work together, unspoken indications that "It's been a lovely day and I'm crazy to go to bed with you," or "It's been a rough day and it would be good to have some sex." These signs are a profound part of stimulation to sexual intercourse. Usually, however, foreplay is taken to mean the stimulating, touching, fondling, cuddling, embracing, and kissing that people do before intercourse, so that is how I'll use the word here.

Volumes have been written about the strictly mechanical, technical aspects of foreplay, which is ironic because the physical maneuvers of foreplay are relatively simple and free. They cannot compare with the complexities of swimming, playing tennis, playing golf, or dancing, let alone driving a car or flying a plane. We can use both hands, one hand, our legs, lips, tongue, sexual organs, any part of us, to touch and caress the person we're making love to. Pleasure in foreplay plays a tremendous role in whether one's sex life is satisfactory or not; so it may sometimes be good to tell a lover where to touch. But people do not need to be taught how to touch. A basic knowledge of anatomy and physiology is helpful to the understanding of what is going on, but is not necessary for performance. Put a healthy, interested, and ready female and a healthy, interested, and ready male near each other, and they will know what to do. It isn't difficult. Foreplay is basically the same the world over. Bodies touch and entwine, hands caress, and mouths kiss various places on the other's body.

Foreplay invites intercourse, sets the stage for it, and gets the body ready for it. But as pleasurable as it is, it is not absolutely necessary. Women can get orgasms without foreplay—even sitting at a desk in an office, for instance—if their thoughts are sufficiently erotic. But women usually require foreplay to come to a sexual climax, and foreplay can arouse a man who is out of the mood for sex. She touches his leg with her fingertips and he gets an erection. Or he kisses her ear and her vagina becomes moist from glandular secretion.

If foreplay becomes stressful, it is usually for psychological reasons. Sometimes physical problems, or basic ignorance seem involved, but this is rare.

First let's consider clumsiness. At some time or other most people are accused of being clumsy in foreplay or intercourse or both, or of being thoughtless and even hurting the other person; but if people care for one another and feel free with one another, they will say what is pleasant and enjoyable and what is uncomfortable or even painful. This is as simple as saying "Ouch, that hurts."

When someone repeatedly finds a lover clumsy, it usually indicates that the lover is not considered attractive or desirable. There is rarely such a thing as simple clumsiness in bed causing a real problem. A person who keeps scratching a lover's genitals while touching them, for instance, has another problem, which most likely is antagonism toward that lover or the opposite sex.

Foreplay or intercourse seldom become stressful simply because of lack of information or misinformation. Such a degree of ignorance is rare today. Very occasionally one partner enters marriage somewhat sexually uninformed and afraid of any sexual activity other than kissing and basic intercourse; this problem can usually be worked through easily if the other partner is tender and patient. Most problems of misinformation turn out to be deeper fears.

Foreplay becomes stressful when, as occasionally happens, one partner or the other insists that it always be done the same way—that it must follow a certain progression or take a certain length of time. It becomes dully ritualistic and mechanical. Or, it can be stressful when, for reasons locked in the psyche of one partner, a couple cannot or does not indulge in foreplay. The reason may be that one partner does not love the other, and wants to get the whole thing over and done with as soon as possible. Or there may be other psychological problems that make foreplay impossible—for instance, a difficulty in giving or receiving pleasure. Foreplay will be stressful when the two partners strongly disagree about what is delicious, charming, and pleasurable to do in bed. There are, in short, numerous kinds of psychological barriers to free and happy foreplay, most of them due to the fact that the sexual partner is not the person the other one wants deeply to be with, relax with, and be intimate with.

Variations. People are fascinated with and curious about intercourse not because there are so many varieties, but because this physiological activity is capable of producing intense, extreme, and powerful feelings that go beyond the actual sexual act. In the first place, there are not so many physical varieties of intercourse. Even if it is defined as putting the erect penis anywhere in the woman's body that it can penetrate, the variety of possible positions in sexual intercourse is still limited. The very anatomy of the penis is limiting. It has no joints, so that its range of possible maneuvers is small. A hand can perform many more actions than an erect penis. Also, there is the matter of size. The average erect penis is thought to be five to seven inches long and from one to one-and-a-half inches in diameter. The penis has to enter a body orifice that can accommodate it, and there are only three orifices in the female body that can: the vagina, the mouth, and the rectum. There are just so many angles from which it can be put into them, and to achieve and give full satisfaction the penis generally has to be moved rhythmically in and out, in and out, which further limits the possible positions. Among other things, this means that those who suggest to people with sexual problems that they "get adventurous and try lots of positions" are suggesting an impossible cure. There are not lots of positions.

Nor is there one fool-proof position. People give simplistic advice. "Man on top of woman is after all the best position," or "Woman on top of man is terrific," or "If you will learn to do it from behind, it will solve all your problems," or "Just try lying on your sides." These statements ignore the fact that what we seek in sexual activity is far more complex than variety in positions and movements. We want the kind of fulfillment only possible from an intense relationship with another person. This tremendously private, physically intimate act is capable of being a strongly ecstatic experience, and that's one reason it's so important.

Intercourse generally means penis in vagina. Ideally it culminates in the stimulation of both partners to the physical and psychological sensations of orgasm at or near the same moment, with, of course, ejaculation by the male. Frequently, in fact, orgasm is not simultaneous, and both lovers do not always reach it. In general, though not always, women need longer stimulation to reach orgasm. Orgasm seems to be equally intense for the two sexes, but a man's ends relatively quickly and his penis gets soft. A woman can maintain some orgiastic sensation considerably longer. In short, physiological differences between male and female affect the way intercourse progresses.

So do the practicalities of daily life. Sometimes the couple has enough time to stimulate to orgasm the woman who cannot reach it in a quick encounter. Sometimes they don't. It is the couple's relationship, however, that is most basic to the quality of their intercourse. Obviously, forty years of married life will not be forty years of simultaneous orgasms. But strong love makes ecstatic emotions well up more easily, and these will stimulate more orgasms.

A male can be sexually stimulated and get an erection from any gentle rhythmic stimulation of his penis. In the course of making love he can have an orgasm and ejaculate almost anywhere—in his hand, in his partner's hand, on her belly, or elsewhere on her body. It used to be believed that it was physiologically harmful to a man to ejaculate outside the vagina, but physiologically it is not harmful at all. Nor are women hurt physiologically by reaching orgasm by means other than vaginal intercourse. Psychologically, it may be different. Sexual activity in which one or both partners usually or always reaches orgasm when the penis is outside the vagina, will be stressful and psychologically difficult.

Sometimes people will do this sort of thing playfully. A man may be very excited by the fact that his wife has an ample belly, or a skinny belly, or a soft belly, or a hard belly, and want to ejaculate on it. He may even specifically like to recline to the right of her and ejaculate on the right side of her belly. Problems with this kind of playful behavior tend to be like the problems that come up in foreplay. One partner may like an activity that, for personal reasons, the other does not desire or even finds repulsive. Frequently, when a man and a woman have trouble with their sex life, they ascribe it to conflict over a certain aspect of their sexual ritual, such as a particular location of ejaculation. Usually, though, there is more to the problem. One partner may be unable to relax and be sexually free and open, and so cannot be sexually successful even with a loved person. Or, more malignantly, one partner may not be aroused by the other partner at all and may not be aware of it; or, for his or her own reasons, may not be willing to admit it.

As for the mechanics of intercourse itself, although the size of the penis varies from man to man, the differences in size are not enormous, and anatomical differences have even less significance in the female. A vagina that is big enough to provide a passageway for a baby to be born can certainly accommodate any erect penis for intercourse. Nor does it matter that one partner is much taller, shorter, heavier, or lighter than the other. Tenderness, attention, and gentleness can keep differences in size and weight from causing discomfort or awkwardness.

The position of man on top of woman is satisfactory for many people. It allows the man to penetrate the vagina deeply. The pressure of his body between the woman's legs stimulates large areas of the perineum, including the clitoris. His hands are free to caress other places. Her hands are free to caress him. She can touch his hands or his cheeks or his shoulders or his back or his scrotum as he thrusts in and out. This position allows face-to-face contact, so that the couple can kiss. Woman on top of man can be equally satisfactory. Some women like it because it gives them more control over clitoral stimulation. Some couples prefer intercourse while lying side to side, and some couples like to have the male penetrate from the back.

It is not the position itself that matters most. If she on top of him is very satisfying and leads to orgasm in both, it is very likely that he on top of her will be very satisfying and will lead to orgasm in both. If intercourse is not stunningly terrific with him on top of her, it is very unlikely to be stunningly terrific with her on top of him. A couple having unsatisfactory vaginal intercourse with the man on top of the woman is deluding themselves if they think reversing positions will fix everything. It is unlikely that their dissatisfaction is either mechanical or due only to boredom or a lack of imagination; it won't disappear if they become more adventurous and try a new position.

While having intercourse, women are more apt to talk to men than vice versa simply because for women, it's easier to talk, because their sexual physiology is more passive initially. Many women like to be talked to by their lovers, but in approaching orgasm, women too may not have any energy left either for talking or listening. After intercourse, having expended much energy and then dropped away from orgasm quickly, men tend to want to roll over and go to sleep. Women, with their capacity for sustained or quickly repeatable orgiastic feeling, tend to want the sex to go on and on. What happens then—consistently, over the years of marriage—is very important to a couple's sexual relationship. If the man will not go on and play a bit more with her, a wife may feel rejected. She's likely to think her husband is a great lover, though, if he keeps some sex play going after they have reached orgasm, or he brings her to orgasm if she hasn't reached it in intercourse. A woman may feel hurt by a man who suddenly turns away after sex. The man may be feeling at that moment that she doesn't appreciate him enough. Both of them do well to say affectionate and reassuring things at the end of sex.

Lingering feelings of discontent after sex can be serious. One partner may have a problem of latent homosexuality. Some depressed people consistently feel, "Is that all?" Sex may fail to gratify because one partner really wanted to be in bed with someone else. If these problems can't be talked about by the partners, it's a sign that psychiatric help may be needed. As long as the two can speak, even haltingly, of anything that is wrong—tonight, this week, this year—there is a good chance that they themselves can make their intercourse better.

Oral Sex. The recent preoccupation with oral sex in our society is so great that you might think it's a fascinating new invention of the twentieth century, which of course it is not. Oral sex is probably as old as sex itself. Two people who are having sex try, in their excitement, to get closer and closer to one another and indeed literally into one another in various ways. Intimate kissing involves more than just the meeting of two sets of lips. Lovers push their tongues from one mouth to the other. Many lovers quite spontaneously move from this to kissing the partner's body and genitals or bring their genitals to the partner's mouth for seeing, kissing, licking, sucking, penetration.

Oral sex is seldom a stress on a marriage. It is not damaging to the woman or to the man. If you put your penis in the mouth of a vicious woman who doesn't like you very much, you run a certain risk that she may take a bite; or a sadistic man may try to injure a woman by biting her genitalia. Therefore don't present your precious genitalia to the mouth of somebody who does not love you or is not at least kindly disposed to you, because you could be physically hurt. Mouth-to-genital contact between people who know and trust one another and are engaged in intense love making is very common, and won't harm potency, fertility, longevity, muscle power, or anything else. It can be very pleasurably sensual. Oral sex, however, is a matter of personal choice and personal style just like other things, and although there are many people who rave about the ecstacy of it, there are others who do not like it. No couple should think that, if their sexual relationship in general leaves a lot to be desired, oral sexuality will ring bells for them and make everything great.

Oral sex becomes stressful when one partner is eager for it and the other is afraid, put off, or bored by it. It is a very intimate, exposed activity, and people who in general are somewhat afraid and hesitant about having sex often find it difficult to allow themselves to relax enough to have oral sex. A man may fear his lover's teeth will hurt his penis, or a woman may not want her lover to smell her genitalia. One partner, expecially one who finds oral sex extremely satisfying, may insist on it, and the other may withold it, so that sex ceases to be a free and warm activity. Furthermore, suggestible people who are insecure about their own sexual styles and preferences are very likely to be impressed by the current popular interest in oral sex and insist on a great deal of it, even if it does not appeal to their sexual partners. The important truth is that, to avoid stress in sex, oral or any other kind, each partner must want to please, and each partner must be free to ask to be pleased.

Anal Sex. The other bodily orifice used for intercourse, the rectum, is penetrated through the anus, which is why it's called anal intercourse. This is also an ancient practice. In some cultures anal intercourse was used as an absolutely foolproof contraceptive method. A lot of people have done it over a long period of time, so obviously many find it pleasureable. There are psychological reasons. First, anal sex is another way to satisfy the sexual desire to get into another person's body. Second, in early childhood, a great deal of action takes place in the area of the rectum and the anus—anal control plays a very important part in childhood development—so there are many sensual memory traces attached to that area. These traces are reactivated in sexual activity. Many people want to sniff, look at, touch, fool around with, and penetrate or have penetrated this previously dominant body area, which is capable of erotic sensations.

Physiologically, mishaps can occur in anal intercourse. The penis is pushed into an orifice that was not constructed to take things in. It is built to expel feces and the rest of the time to stay closed. The penis has to push past the sphincter muscle that keeps the anus closed, and sometimes inflicts pain as it does. Also, the rectum does not have lubricating glands; the penis is pushed into a dry opening, with some danger that the tissues will be painfully torn. Pain and abrasion can be avoided with gentleness and the use of some lubricant; or by the woman learning to relax so the man can penetrate more easily. When she is relaxed, the sphincter does not resist opening nearly as much.

Anal intercourse has the same limitations as other sexual activities. It is not going to make a couple more or less sensual, liberated, or loving, If they enjoy everything else together, they are likely to enjoy this too. If they share nothing before they start anal intercourse, they are not going to have anything special during or after it, except that maybe the woman will have a sore bottom.

It has been my clinical experience that more men are interested in anal sex than women. Some men, but more women, find this mode of sexuality the least appealing; some men, but more women, find it unpleasant or even repulsive, even discounting the woman's greater chance of physical pain. Not every dislike is a neurosis or phobia to be attacked with vigor and conquered, and disliking anal intercourse makes some sense. After all, the rectum has a basic function that is not sexual. Through it we eliminate our waste products, which are messy, smelly, and loaded with bacteria. The rectum and the anus have associations that have nothing to do with tenderness and sexual love. In the heat of sexual excitement a person may find the partner's anus exciting, touchable, sniffable, lickable; but the partner, if not at that moment at the same pitch of excitement, may find it all unappetizing.

The wish for anal intercourse for some is also apt to include an element of wishing to degrade the partner. There are men who will engage in it as a sort of cruel sexual joke, a dirty trick, and then taunt the woman later on.

Alcohol and Marriage. Some chemical substances that people use to try to stimulate themselves can be sexually harmful—namely, alcohol and drugs. The harm done is directly related to the quantity used and the frequency of use. Alcohol and drugs are toxic and may become addictive. Since many drugs are illegal, the user also faces the risk of ingesting a potent substance whose composition and purity are not known. Occasionally drinking small quantities of alcohol or taking some other mild chemical relaxant is clearly not devastating, but regular and heavy use can be another story.

Alcohol depresses the functioning of the central nervous system. As we drink more, we progressively lose the capacity to do the things the central nervous system enables us to do. The highest, most subtle mental functions are depressed first, and the moods that are right underneath them, perhaps being held in check by conscious judgment, come out. A man and wife who are out for dinner, enjoying seeing each other alone for a change, may become relaxed and giggly when they drink, and then have some especially exhilarating sex. No harm done. But if one of the couple feels resentment or anger at something the other one did, they are likely to fight instead. Alcohol next impairs the power of judgment, as when a drinker makes disparaging remarks about his boss at a party. Then we lose fine and gross muscle coordination; our speech gets slurred, and we start to stagger. Finally, we pass out.

Along the way, our ability to function sexually also progressively decreases. This decrement is more obvious in men; a man who's been drinking has trouble getting and maintaining an erection. Alcohol seriously adds to any problems of impotence he might already have. Women too have appreciable difficulties having sex when they are drunk. It's harder for them to maintain their interest and stay involved, which they need to do to make it likely that they will reach orgasm.

Alcohol is often used as a sedative, to relieve anxiety about sex in general or some specific kind of sexual activity—fellatio, for example—or to cover up an aversion to the partner. Drunk people are generally less aware of what's happening to them or with whom it's happening. In a dazed fashion they somehow go on and get through the sexual act. If their anxiety is relieved by the drinking, they think it has stimulated them sexually. That is not a healthy way to have sex. A drunk person is not a skilled or sensitive lover; he or she is a lousy lover. Anyone who regularly has to use alcohol to deaden sexual misery or to feel sexually stimulated has a serious sexual problem.

People do not slip into alcoholism by chance, but as a consequence of other problems—business problems, love problems, inability to handle a job, and so on. Alcoholics are tense, troubled people who think drinking can ease their troubles. To the extent that their drinking dominates them, they are weak marital partners. Some people seem to seek out alcoholics to marry. People who fall in love with alcoholics and marry them often do so to satisfy their own hidden needs. Alcoholism is a powerful, self-perpetuating adjustment to life, and it is often impossible for one loving person to rescue an alcoholic.

Sometimes two drunks find each other, or one spouse becomes an alcoholic in the course of drinking to keep the other one company. As a result of sharing this totally unrealistic life style, they may get along better temporarily but they will go down hill together very fast.

People married to alcoholics sometimes cajole, and sometimes threaten them; one or the other of these approaches occasionally works. Sometimes the miserable sober spouse brings in someone from outside the marriage—a much-loved brother, a priest, a rabbi, a powerful uncle. A psychiatrist may be called. Alcoholics Anonymous, with its structure of mutual support for alcoholics trying to beat their addiction, helps some of them a great deal. A lot of help usually is needed. Alcoholics are people with very low frustration tolerance—immature, insecure, wanting instant relief and release. They tend to demand almost constant attention, and most spouses can't give it. An alcoholic may have to be sent to an organization that is equipped to really take over his or her life.

One kind of alcoholic relationship is illustrated by Susan's second marriage.

Both her husbands have been alcoholics, as was her father. Susan remembers her father mostly as a charming, fun-loving man with boyish good looks, who was always laughing. Her mother, however, used to say "A handsome man with a drinking problem is no good." Susan remembers her mother as irritable, demanding, and complaining, although actually she was probably depressed and overworked. As a child, Susan blamed her mother for her father's drinking problem; she was sure that if her mother only took better care of her appearance and was cheerful and kept the house better, her father would stay at home and not drink. As an adult, Susan has spent her life trying to prove she was right.

She met her first husband in college. He drank a lot, but she ignored it, and thought that once they were married he would stop. She met her second husband through her first husband; they had become friends at AA. He also is a handsome, charming man. Twice now, Susan has tried to prove that she could do better than her mother, and that indeed her beloved father was not at fault. She is still convinced that the right wife can keep any man from drinking. So far she's failed twice. She's taken upon herself a responsibility that belongs with the other person.

Kate's story is different. Her second husband is an alcoholic. Her first husband had cancer. When she met her first husband in college, he told her that he was ill and was therefore a bad marital risk. Kate was a shy girl who didn't think she was particularly attractive, vivacious, bright, or interesting; her first husband made her feel good about herself. He encouraged her to dress stylishly and to participate in school activities. It never occurred to her that she could have achieved any of this without him and, in gratitude, she married him. They were happy for six years and then he died. Kate missed him desperately and was deeply depressed for a long time.

She met her second husband in a bar. She had reentered the singles scene with little hope that she would be successful, that she would attract anyone. She was delighted when a handsome man picked her up. He showered her with attention, and the romance progressed rapidly. Kate was aware that Henry drank too much but, because she was so appreciative, she could not bring herself to reject his proposal.

Sometimes it is marriage and its responsiblities that bring out an incipient alcoholism. Jeannie, for instance, is an alcoholic unable to cope with her life as a wife and mother. She has two girls, ages seven and five; Tom, her husband, manages a shoe store. He comes home to a dirty house where dinner is not ready. His two little girls have to fend for themselves and are often left alone. Jeannie was a pretty, slim, blonde girl, almost childlike, Tom used to think, in her gentleness; now she's a cranky, cantankerous, discontented, irritable woman looking for a fight.

The same qualities that Tom found so appealing when Jeannie was eighteen underlie her alcoholism. In those days, she would hang around with a group of young people at the shopping center where Tom worked as a shoe salesman. He saw her as having a charming, childlike naivete that appealed to his masculinity. He thought he would take care of her. Actually, she was a tense girl from an unhappy home who was trying to escape from her frustrations and anger. What kept her symptoms under control was essentially that she had no responsibilities. She did not take school seriously, she didn't have a job, and she escaped her home problems by hanging around with her friends in an adolescent, make-believe world.

Tom thought she was a cheerful, happy-go-lucky, carefree girl who'd make a marvelous wife and balance his somewhat serious and shy personality. He was aware even then that she seemed to drink a lot of beer. She always had a cigarette in her mouth and cheerfully admitted that she smoked pot whenever she could get her hands on it. Tom took all this to mean that Jeannie was simply someone who loved parties. After they married and had to live within Tom's salary, Jeannie found the restrictions and the responsibilities unbearable, especially after the children were born. She no longer could run to the shopping center to be with her friends to escape her anxieties, and she turned more and more to alcohol to help her get through the day.

Drugs. By and large, the so-called recreational drugs that people take for pleasure are also detrimental to sexual performance and enjoyment. They may, like alcohol, dampen anxiety about sex. Many of these drugs are extremely destructive. The hallucinogens, L.S.D. (lysergic acid diethylamide) and P.C.P. (phencyclidine or "angel dust") tend to make sex seem irrelevant.

We occasionally hear that people who are fairly well off emotionally and inclined toward sexual experimentation may take a little L.S.D. or even P.C.P. and report that their sexual inhibitions are loosened; but these drugs are seldom used for sex alone and reports of their aphrodisiac potential are false. L.S.D. and P.C.P. are strong hallucinogens, extremely dangerous, and should *never* be used. Furthermore, people who use drugs for sex are hardly ever anxiety free to start with, so they usually take more than a little; the drug's other effects take over and they can't perform sexually at all.

Marijuana can make people a little braver sexually, but people who smoke a lot of pot typically lose their motivation for sex, as well as other activities. Continued use of the opiate heroin reduces all drives. Female heroin addicts become frigid and many even do not menstruate; male addicts often become impotent. People who sniff cocaine say it's good for sex; but any sexual help comes in the early stages of use and is only due to disinhibition. Heavy use of cocaine can lead to severe mental debilitation, as can amphetamine abuse.

Physiological tolerance for alcohol and drugs quickly increases with regular use, so that larger and larger quantities are needed to achieve the desired effects. The toxicity of these substances is directly related to the quantity ingested; this means that the problems resulting from using them also increase. Under the influence of alcohol and drugs, the ability to function deteriorates in all areas including the ability to stay interested and involved in an active sex life.

Psychologically and pragmatically, the process can be devastating to a marriage. A spouse who has developed a dependence on drink or some drug, and finds it essential for getting through the day, may try to convince the other spouse that it's harmless, only a matter of personal taste. "Join the party," he or she says. If the spouse does, it's never a party for long.

Pornography. Pornographic books, pictures, and movies are fairly commonly used for sexual stimulation in marriage.

There's no harm in them, unless you have a strong need to look at images of other sex objects every time you make love with your spouse, which does indicate rather clearly that you feel you don't have the ideal sex object in bed with you. If your spouse becomes aware of how you feel, it will be hurtful. But if pornography arouses one partner and the other isn't hurt by it, or if both realize that they like pornographic material or need it for excitement, they aren't harming each other.

Problems arise when one partner enjoys the use of pornography and the other is hurt or revolted by it. Pornography is widely available today, and many people are curious about it and occasionally enjoy it. Couples may now and then go to a pornographic movie partly to get a little titillation and partly just for another experience of the world. This doesn't mean that either one is dissatisfied with their partner. Indeed, for a spouse to be extremely revolted or terrified at the idea of this kind of sightseeing may be somewhat inappropriate. In the context of a married couple's intimate life, one partner may correctly feel betrayed and dehumanized by pornography if the other finds it essential to their sex life.

Sadomasochism. Such acts as applying pressure on jugular veins, beating, binding with ropes or straps, or forcing objects like bottles into bodily orifices are not in any way a true part of sexual activity. To want to perform such dangerous acts and to consider them sexual activity indicates deep-seated psychological problems. Sadists, the people who have such desires, have serious conflicts about their sexual identity and about relating to other people in love as well as in other areas. They use sex to express their resentment, hostility, and destructiveness toward a world into which they feel they do not fit. Masochists, the people who welcome such acts or at least allow them to be done to them, are also psychologically troubled.

Something degrading or dangerous may be done to you once or twice, but if you care about yourself, you start doing all you can to change your situation.

Playful, imaginative sex between two trusting people rather often gets vigorous and aggressive, even to the point of someone pinching or squeezing or biting too hard. But then, if the other partner says, "Hey, that hurts," the first becomes gentler.

Something very different happens in sadomasochistic sex. One person is using sexual activity to gain mastery and power over another by insisting on performing violent or at least degrading acts. These activities are an outlet for the dominating person's fantasies of conflict, violence, and power.

Sadistic maneuvers are often expressions of a mutual power struggle that runs through a couple's whole relationship. One partner may be sadistically dominant in bed, the other sadistically cruel in some other area of life, for a person who can be sadistic can also be masochistic. Whatever its dynamics in a particular couple's life, sadomasochism in sex and other areas of married life is not only cruel, but terribly sad and destructive.

Illness. Organic illnesses or injuries can cause sexual dysfunction. In men, injury to the spinal cord, urological disease, or some endocrine disease is often the cause of impotence or weak potency. In women, some local condition such as a tumor in the pelvic area may cause obstruction or pressure; a neurological problem like paralysis may prevent movement of the legs; endocrine disease may cause atrophy and therefore pain in the vaginal area. Any organic condition that causes severe sexual dysfunction, has to be serious, advanced, and incapacitating in other areas as well, and the diagnosis is very rarely made on the basis of sexual dysfunction alone. Illness brings with it more than sexual stress, of course, but, for the people involved, the stress of the sexual dysfunction is added to the stress of all the other problems arising from the illness.

As I have already discussed, psychosexual illnesses may make people avoid sex. Springing from deep psychological problems, psychosexual illnesses do not have the physical definiteness of organic disease, but they are bona fide illnesses that can afflict women and men with sexual difficulties with all or most partners and under all or most circumstances. Let me emphasize that they are not deliberate acts of one partner to reject or degrade the other. They cause stress on the marriage as other illnesses cause stress on the marriage and, require professional help to cure. They show themselves in men as various degrees of impotence, and also as problems with ejaculation. These latter problems may range from getting aroused and ejaculating before they've had time to start having intercourse, to taking a very long time to ejaculate, or not being able to do it at all, even with an erection. In women, these illnesses show themselves as various degrees of frigidity; in extreme cases, dyspareunia, which is painful intercourse, or vaginismus, which is a spasm of the pelvic musculature and the lower third of the vagina that makes penetration impossible.

People who are afflicted by disease, organic or psychological, have a great advantage if they have a stable, secure, and sustaining marriage, which means, in this context, that their spouse does everything possible to help them toward some degree of sexual functioning and pleasure. Fortunately, these are not common diseases. The vast majority of men can feel sexually stimulated and get an erection; the vast majority of women are sexually alive and interested, and their vaginas get lubricated and are easily penetrable under a great many circumstances and with no problems at all.

Sex Manuals. There are many books on sexual technique. They range from frankly pornographic books full of drawings or action photos that are used by many couples for arousing themselves when all else fails, to medical manuals of greater or lesser scientific validity. Lots of them, particularly the ones on technique, go into endless mechanical, physiological, and anatomical detail. This voluminous literature sells; the demand for sex manuals and other guidance books is unending. Frustrated and unfulfilled people hope that somewhere they will find some correct formula, a definite plan with definite steps to follow, a technique so good that no matter who uses it or with whom, full sexual satisfaction will result. Unfortunately, it doesn't happen like that. There's no getting away from it; when there is a sexual problem, almost always the issue is not just what you do, but with whom you do it and under what circumstances, and how you respond to each other totally, technique and all. Books may promise that you can solve problems by mastering the mechanical aspects of sex. But, in my experience, it is very, very rare that a sexual problem can be corrected through mechanical adjustments alone.

Sex therapy clinics are another mirage. They are designed to deal directly and quickly with the problems people have in bed with each other. Couples go to clinics to try to learn how to achieve an orgasm or how to have a better orgasm, sometimes through having sex with surrogate partners. Such sex therapy is esentially only a new form of adult recreation and a passing fad. The people who practice it have done something useful in enlarging the world's knowledge about sexuality, and most people who undergo it come away feeling more at ease with sex. They can talk of it more easily; they may have more of it. If a couple has a good over-all relationship before they go into sex therapy, they may afterwards have somewhat better sex. But if their over-all relationship is not good, the results are not good, either. Direct sex therapy won't improve a sexual relationship in a troubled marriage because you have to work on the whole relationship, the whole marriage. An essentially mechanical approach is never enough.

People grow, change, and develop sexually—they learn new ways and try new positions. They can do these things on their own. In our anything but easy-going culture, some people need help to relax and be able to indulge in sexual activity. Physiological mechanisms are very much under the control of emotions and, in tense, upset, anxious people, physiological activities of all kinds are disturbed; this includes eating, elimination, sleeping, and sex. Such people need help with their tension and anxiety, not their sexuality.

It's useful to know the physiology of foreplay, of intercourse, of impregnation, of contraception, of pregnancy, and of labor and childbirth. Similarly, it is helpful to know the facts of normal sexuality, and that means knowing what is sexually and sensually stimulating and the truth about sexual facts.

The anatomy of the external sexual organs is rather simple compared to the anatomy of some other organs, they can be touched and examined by hand. The vagina can also be examined. This is a start toward practical anatomical knowledge. After all, people have been having sex from prehistoric times without the benefits of the anatomical labels that we use today or full knowledge of the physiology of the sexual organs. They simply did what came naturally, and that of course is what is still being done.

This seems to me an absolutely central truth. So many of the people who talk a lot about how sex is a normal and natural act are the very same ones who feel that it has to be taught, formally taught, taught in school, no less, to children or adolescents to help them have a successful adult sex life! Why do we not have to teach our children how to swallow or how to breathe?

Teaching sex formally in school is of very little value in preventing adult sexual problems. Stress in sexual activity is seldom due to lack of knowledge or faulty knowledge. Frightening misinformation about sex can be damaging to sexual performance, but usually only when it is learned in such a way that the fear becomes incorporated into the child's very being—that is, when the misinformation was acquired through an experience that was a trauma to the developing personality. If that happens, formal teaching will not help, treatment is necessary. Most other misconceptions can be easily unlearned, and most people do unlearn them through experience.

Sex is tantalizing, pleasurable, and readily available. Even little children find out about it, and they are very eager to share their information with one another. Each generation of children receives a substantial part and probably the most enjoyable part of its sex education from its peers. The information obtained in this way is often erroneous. Although this form of education also often involves some practical demonstrations, it is still almost never harmful unless some other factors become part of such experiences; factors such as teasing, molestation by older children or adolescents, or being caught at these activities by adults who frightened or punished them in a brutal way.

Where, then, do most adult sexual problems come from? The main source of adult sexual problems is the complex area, not amenable to simple methods of education and indoctrination, of unhappy early relationships between children and their parents and, most importantly, unhappy relationships between parents that children observe.

Conflict-free adult sexuality comes from having been the happy child of a happy marriage where the parents, although not directly observed by the children in sexual activity, indicated clearly to the children that an important reason for their affection for one another was that one was male and the other female and they were sexually fulfilled and satisfied. The parents did not need a high level of technical sexual knowledge which they then easily, or in a scholarly fashion, imparted to their offspring. They were simply open and easy with each other and clearly affectionate and happy with one another.

CHAPTER 4

Children in Marriage

CONTRACEPTION

A major reason why all societies in all periods of history have had rules about entering into and maintaining marriage, as well as dissolving it, has been to protect the children who are necessary for society's survival. Societies reward people who have and raise children within a marriage, and punish those who have children outside marriage. This societal approval for having children is one of the major reasons for getting married. Nonetheless, I believe you should decide whether for your *own* reasons you want to have children or not, taking into account the consequences of the decision and your own potential and limitations.

Safe and effective contraceptive devices make it possible to choose whether–and when–to have children. To find which method of contraception is best for you, consult a doctor. The hormonal medication for women known as "the pill" is a very effective method; like other powerful medications it can produce some side effects, but when it is appropriately prescribed and used as prescribed, it is a safe medication. So far there is no chemical contraceptive device for men.

The diaphragm for women and the condom for men are effective mechanical methods. The diaphragm has been used by millions of women with very satisfactory results. Condoms are also commonly used, although some men do complain that they cut down on sensation. The various kinds of foams for insertion into the vagina are not as effective. The use of an intrauterine device, although effective, can have serious side effects and therefore should be undertaken only after consultation with a doctor. There has so far been no contraceptive device invented that is ideal, otherwise everybody would be using it.

Sterilization is now widely used. In women, it is done by tubal ligation—that is, tying the fallopian tubes. For men, tying the seminal ducts accomplishes the same purpose and is called a vasectomy. These procedures are essentially irreversible. Techniques do exist for reversing them, but these are successful in only a small percentage of cases. Provided people understand and accept its consequences, sterilization can be used for permanent contraception without severe psychological stress. For those whose religious principles prohibit the use of contraceptive devices or sterilization, the rhythm method gives a good deal of control over conception. Whatever method you decide on should permit you to feel comfortable.

What about abortion? Abortion is a safe medical procedure. On the other hand, it is a surgical procedure, and does have the potential for complications. It is not an acceptable form of contraception. Considering that thousands of women have had abortions and have then gone on to conceive again and have children, abortion cannot be viewed as devastating. But it always evokes strong feelings, and even women who have had several abortions typically vow after each one that they will never again put themselves in a situation where they will need another one. An abortion is a psychologically serious event, and demands careful thought about the meaning of the pregnancy.

Decisions about having or not having children have a great bearing on whether adult life is going to be happy and successful or not. I am not saying that you must have children to be happy, but simply that a decision to have or not to have them has far-reaching consequences. Parents' relationships with their children are among the richest, most rewardng, and most enduring of life. On the other hand, raising children is a very difficult and arduous task, and some adults who take the time to think it through choose, rightly for themselves, not to have children.

MARRIAGE AND CHILDREN

In raising children, these facts above all stand undisputed: more troubled and failing children come from unhappy homes than from happy homes, and more healthy and successful children come from happy homes than from unhappy ones. And in general, the happiest homes are those at whose center is a successful, healthy marriage.

There are two major sets of factors that make a good marriage a good setting in which to raise children—the practical and the emotional. The practical factors are those that guarantee the infant's survival—its needs for food, shelter, clothing, and protection for years and years, twenty-four hours a day, seven days a week. To satisfy these demands for even one child requires much time and energy and considerable material resources. It is a great advantage to have two people devoted to the children's welfare, since for one parent to raise children is a Herculean task. It is hard enough to do all the housekeeping and homemaking chores; it's even harder to do those and go out to work, as most single parents must do. Financial considerations are not all-important in raising children, since children do turn out well under the most diversified economic conditions. Still, poverty is debilitating, to parents as well as children. Furthermore, to grow up in a one-parent household for whatever reason—death, separation, illness, divorce, desertion—increases the chance of physical danger to a child, since there is much less adult strength and stamina available to protect the children.

On the other hand, just being able to take good care of all of a child's physical and material needs will not guarantee a healthy setting. The emotional environment children grow up in is of paramount importance to their healthy development. Everyone needs to feel loved by at least someone, preferably by a lot of people. And children especially need to feel loved, because only when they're sure of being loved can they feel secure. They know they must be taken care of and they feel, correctly, that it will be forthcoming only from people who love them. Children don't need to have all their whims fulfilled to feel loved. They have to feel accepted for themselves, sure that they will be well taken care of, and know their environment is stable. Security to children means they don't fear abandonment or other harm. Without that security they cannot grow and develop in a healthy way. Too much of their energy goes into anxiety, which robs them of the chance to develop their potential as human beings—to acquire skills, to observe the world and learn about it, to establish and maintain relationships, to learn to get along with other people, all of which they want to do to prepare themselves for adulthood.

Children also need to love the people who love them. This is another most important factor in the formation of a healthy personality, because it teaches them they have something to give that clearly is worth a great deal to others. To have a lot of this receiving and giving of love taken away by the death of a parent, for instance, is one of the greatest tragedies of childhood. It marks the personality and leaves scars there forever, and makes a child feel much less secure, with a feeling of sadness that never entirely goes away.

Starting with the central early exchange of love—or, sadly, lack of it—a child's personality is formed gradually and slowly by the interaction of the growing human organism and its environment. The parenting adult or adults have more control over the child's environment than anybody else. To a large extent they provide and interpret the environment to the child. Thus these adults, who are usually the mother and father, have the largest impact on the child's personality. Why is it such a good thing for these people actually to be the mother and father, and happily married to each other?

To begin with, for healthy emotional development, a child needs both loving, kindly female and male figures in the environment; most importantly, one key woman and one key man. We find our sexual identity as children through our interactions with people of both sexes; thus a boy needs to test what it means to be male, a girl what it means to be female, and they need stable relationships with other people of both sexes to do it. Nothing gives children this experience as well as living in a house with two key adults, one male and one female, who have a close, secure, and sexual relationship—and there is no better setting for such a relationship than marriage.

A good marriage is beneficial in another, broader way. Children learn by copying, by imitating. To learn how to get along with others, children need an opportunity to see others doing it in various contexts. If both parents are there, a child can observe and evaluate how they treat him or her, as well as how they relate to one another and their environment. From these observations the child develops a picture of himself or herself and also a picture of the world. The child also tests his or her own observations about the world against the parents' reactions. In other words, the parents are the child's most prominent, readily available, and therefore most important models. How they relate to the child and to one another will influence the child's relationships throughout life—important, deep relationships, such as that with a mate sometime in the future, and all superficial relationships, as well.

Fortunate, then, are children who grow up in the setting of a marriage where the parents' relationship, including the sexual part of it, works well, and there is lots of love for the children.

This doesn't mean that the parents will never fight. Nor does it mean the children should never see the parents fight. I think it is a big mistake to keep children from seeing that. What children need, rather, is to be shown by example how adults cope with stresses, disappointments, hard work, joys, vacations, recreation, fun, love, quarrels, and making up after quarrels, and to see and learn how adults show pleasure, displeasure, anger, and affection. The chances of the child having emotional problems are increased by living in an unhappy home, where these emotional experiences are distorted, or by living in a single-parent household, where they are relatively absent. Neither setting can develop a good picture of a normal happy home life. Children from such homes have trouble with close relationships because they do not believe that they can be achieved or even exist, or they overidealize them. This means, in turn, that throughout life, close relationships will fail to live up to these ideals, so that they have great problems maintaining them.

WHY AND WHEN TO HAVE CHILDREN

Children can become a serious stress on a marriage when the partners undertake to have them without comprehending either what parenting will mean to themselves, or its serious consequences. To say "let's have a baby," or "I want to have a baby," doesn't take into account that having a baby is only a very short phase in the unending relationship with a child. People should know why they want to have children, what they hope to accomplish by it, and how the children will change their life style, including what they will have to forgo for the children. And each prospective parent's understanding of the issues related to having children needs to be acceptable to the other one.

Basically, the right reason for people to have children is simply that they want to have them. The qualifying factors are that they also understand what it means to be parents and they are willing and able to handle the consequences in a mature, responsible manner. Beyond this, different people want children for different particular reasons. The variety of hopes and fantasies that different people hope to fulfill in having children is wide indeed. Nobody has the right to sit in judgment and dictate who should have children, or for what reasons anybody should have children, though some reasons are realistic and others are not.

Many people have children in an attempt to approach immortality. The world's literature is full of examples of children symbolizing their parents' hope of immortality. People don't gain immortality by having children, but children seem somehow to fulfill a deep wish of many people that part of them and their ancestors should continue. People have children to avoid loneliness, to have somebody to love and be loved by. People have children because they offer the possibility of a close human relationship extending over many years. People have children for security, to have someone on whom they can depend, particularly in old age. Of course, no one can be sure they'll actually get security or long-lasting human contact from children; still, these are perfectly legitimate reasons to have them. Nor is a reason such as "to carry on my name," with its implications of immortality, to be scorned or mocked. Just about any reason is all right if the parents are willing to devote themselves lovingly to their children and spend the necessary time and energy and money to raise them. But perhaps the most mature and healthy reason for having children is simply that you love to be around them, to marvel at the wonderful process of their growth, and you feel that a life that children are part of is more interesting and vital.

A husband and wife may have different reasons for wanting children, and if having children is not to become stressful, they must accept each other's reasons. It is not essential that they have the same reasons or that both want children with the same intensity. It is important that, since having children is a long-term commitment, the partners both want children, and that both are willing to raise the children that they jointly put on this earth. The undertaking to have children should be a joint project. By the time a man and wife embark on parenthood, both should be committed to it, and each should be aware of the kind and degree of commitment of the other. If the couple has not jointly agreed to parenthood–if one has cajoled, bullied, bribed, blackmailed, or tricked the other into having a child–the child will become a serious stress on the marriage.

The desire to have children may be very strong, and the desire not to have children may be equally strong. Both sets of feelings stem not only from deliberate conscious considerations, but also from the unconscious considerations that are rooted in early childhood and so are powerful and difficult to alter. It is always stressful when the desires of one spouse are the opposite of the other's in this regard. This particular disharmony in the lives of the partners, involving as it does such deep and intense motives, is exceptionally dangerous to the well-being of a marriage. Indeed the issue is often beyond resolution, and many marriages break up over it.

When to have children? What is the ideal time of life for this?

There is a biological limitation on women. When they cease to menstruate, women are no longer able to have children. The average age for this is about forty-eight, with the range of ages very roughly forty-five to fifty-five. But also, as they approach forty, women's chances of having an impaired child increase. For this reason doctors today tend to recommend that every pregnant woman over thirty-five undergo amniocentesis to test the fetus for genetic defects. Some amniotic fluid, which normally contains some cells of the child, is taken from the pregnant woman. Then these cells are grown in a culture, and their chromosomes are examined for defects. If a defect is found—the most usual one is Down's syndrome, a defect of physical and mental development—the pregnancy can be terminated. This problem complicates the issue of childbearing for older women a good deal.

It is also less advisable for men in advanced years to have children than it is for young men. Older men will have less strength to be active fathers, and are more likely to die while their children are still young; but men do not have any age-related cessation of the ability to reproduce. These limitations aside, there is no set age at which people should have children. Any time that a couple is ready and willing to fulfill the parental obligations and not rebel against them is an appropriate time for them; this varies from couple to couple.

Parental challenges today are quite different from those of a few generations ago. Science and technology have given us more choices, and made us more aware of the implications of what we choose. Our life styles are more complicated. Work itself has become more cerebral and abstract. Even simple housekeeping tasks mean we have to know how to run machines safely, and unskilled jobs require the ability to read and do simple math. To bring up children who will be able to cope healthily and successfully with complicated demands is a great challenge—not merely to train them to do the jobs, but also to provide an environment for healthy psychological development, without which training and education will be largely useless. This parental task is made both possible and pressing by the fact that children learn more by watching and imitating the adults around them than they do by being taught directly. So whatever rules people live by, good or bad, are likely to be instilled in their children.

Most people undertake the job of parenthood with the best intentions toward their children; with the aspiration of helping them become happy, fulfilled adults. The desire to have children is so strong for many people that they will have them under circumstances that are a lot less than ideal, which is all right if they also understand that raising them is apt to be especially complicated and difficult. Others are unlikely to have them if times are particularly difficult. The most important determinant of successful parenthood, however, is an honest awareness and realistic appraisal of your own and your spouse's psychological ability to cope with our ever-changing world while raising children.

Children who grow up and develop happily and successfully are a great joy and enrich a marriage tremendously. Children who do not develop well—who run into psychological problems and become unhappy—bring stress into the marriage. To have children bring joy rather than pain, parents must understand how to make marriage a supportive environment, and try to set up such an environment before the children arrive. Otherwise a child arrives in a marriage that is already stressed or is otherwise not right to raise a child in, so that the child runs a sizable risk of developing serious personal problems. If this happens, the child becomes stressful to live with and harder to bring up. The result may be a severely emotionally disturbed child whose parents are under severe psychological stress and may in some cases have to change their whole life in order to take care of the child.

There are advantages and disadvantages to a couple having children while young, fairly young, or approaching middle age. Young parents usually have plenty of energy, which is certainly an advantage. Young people may be financially insecure, and that can be a disadvantage, but what's much more serious is that young parents may not have finished their own maturation process. Many young parents are still struggling with their identity problems, and still need time to explore what they want to do. If they're raising children at the same time that they're struggling to establish and clarify their own identities, the conflicting pressures for time, energy, and resources are very likely to prove overwhelming, unless they know how to allocate time efficiently. Parents with diversified interests and many demands on their time can of course still be excellent parents. But parents who still haven't quite found themselves, who are very insecure about commitment, who are still trying many activities or maybe even experimenting with different lifestyles, may not be ready for parenthood. The continual shifting of gears usually means that less time will be spent with the child and that the quality of that time will be inconsistent. If a young mother feeds her young child regularly one week, but the next week reads all day and feeds the child irregularly, the child may be quite confused—and perhaps be hungry a lot of the time.

People who are ready for the long-term commitment of having children have made peace, or at least realized the need to make peace, with their potential and their limitations. This realization is not necessarily directly tied to a person's chronological age. Ideally this process begins in adolescence and is finished in early adulthood, but someone who continues to have identity problems into the adult years, will experience difficulty in being a parent regardless of age.

People aren't ready to have children until they are willing to accept and live with the fact that a child takes time and energy, and that they have to be willing to expend a great deal of effort and physical and emotional strength on rearing that child. No longer will they be able to spend all their time and energy on their own interests. Infants and young children need safe and appropriate supervision twenty-four hours a day, and it is the responsibility of the parents to make sure that they get it. Not all the time has to be spent with one or both parents, of course. Other arrangements for this supervision can be made, depending on circumstances, preferences, family connections, and finances. However, it is the parents' responsibility to see that no child of theirs is left unattended, and no matter what arrangements people make to have others take care of their children, they themselves need to be willing to spend substantial amounts of time with them.

People also are not ready to have children until they are willing to accept the fact that substantial amounts of their money will have to be spent on them—their food, clothes, shelter, and education. It's not the amount of money that matters. Children are raised happily on limited incomes, and children are raised unhappily on substantial incomes and even fortunes. Some relatively poor people do not feel their children are a financial burden, and some quite well-to-do people feel they are. What is necessary is that prospective parents be aware that they will have to adjust their life style to their children.

The willingness to share is basic. Unless people are willing to share their finances and time and energy with their children, they will consider the children as depriving them of these things and adding serious stress to their lives. The best parents give generously and freely and accept as their reward the growth and development of the child. Those who can't manage this may give resentfully and find their marriages severely stressed. Or they may take another route and neglect the child. Very young parents may think that having a child is a game, that the child is a toy they can play with when convenient and put away when they are busy with other things. But one does not have to be young to neglect children. Older parents who are very involved in their work or social life and do not want to spend the time, money, and effort required for child rearing also often are neglectful.

How to space the children? A couple may decide to have their children very close together because they want the children to be playmates, or because they want to have all their children within a short span of time so that they can return to other activities they have postponed, such as study or travel. An older couple who want several children must perforce have them quickly. There are equally good reasons for having children further apart. A couple who have to depend exclusively on themselves to take care of their children may want each child to be somewhat independent before they undertake the next one. Or they may want to spend the major part of their adult life raising children and therefore decide to spread them out. The key consideration should be that every child is able to have its share of family resources—physical, emotional, and financial. Any new child—second or third or fourth or fifth—will bring new demands on the family. It's not that the second child is double work or half the work of the first one, or that three children are no more effort than two. Each and every child has to be raised with love and devotion, and the parents must provide them.

A couple should feel physically well enough to cope again with the hours, getting up at night, the diapers, the feedings. The chances of being able to provide financially for the new child should seem bright. Both parents should greet the arrival of a new child as a happy event. Is the mother quite willing to bear another child or does she view it with dread? How about her commitments to her husband, her other children, her other interests? Does she fear another child will keep her away from them? Is the father willing to have another child? Will he view it as a rival taking away his wife's attention and interest? How is the couple's sex life? Is it vigorous enough so that the added physical burden of taking care of another baby will not drain them and make their sex life dwindle to very little or nothing at all? How is the father's relationship with the other children? Does he find time to spend with the children who are already in the family? Will he find the time to play with his new child—to talk to, listen to, guide the new child? What are the father's feelings about his work? Does he feel successful? Will he view the new child as an added joy in his life or as a new responsibility that will require him to work longer hours? Will he view this child as a competitor for time he wants to give to work or other personal interests?

The needs of any other child or children should also be taken into account. Are they ready to share the mother's and father's attention with a new child? Are their needs taken care of, so that it will not seem to be a big blow to have another child in the family? Is one of them going through a particularly difficult time, so that it might be wiser to postpone bringing in another sibling? I am not suggesting that children are to be consulted on whether to have more children. The decision to have more children is a decision only for the parents to make. A couple may decide to have more children in spite of the fact or even because of the fact that a child they already have has physical or emotional problems, even if the problems are serious. They may hope to add an untroubled child to their family. Such a choice may work out well and bring the couple much happiness, provided they have thought it through, realize they are adding to an already abnormally large burden, and are willing to help one another fulfill this new commitment.

Then there is the matter of other close family relationships—aunts, uncles, cousins, grandparents. These are important with the first child and every child thereafter. In undertaking to have more children, parents should consider their commitments to other people of importance in their lives. Many of us have complicated commitments to relatives, to the people who raised us and with whom we grew up. Relatives play a great part in building our value systems, setting our priorities in life, developing our strengths and weaknesses. Commitments to relatives vary a great deal. Situations in which commitments to relatives are so powerful as to keep people from having any children at all are rare; but after the first-born, such commitments increasingly become an issue that cannot and should not be ignored.

There is another important consideration related to the extended family. In previous generations members of the extended family tended to be closely and intensely involved in rearing and taking care of children. They pooled their resources so the children could be raised, and everyone's regular adult work—around the family farm, for instance—could continue. Many adults have memories of being raised not only by parents but by grandparents, aunts and uncles, older cousins, and other relatives. The school for parenthood we all attend is our own childhood; consequently, when some of these people picture themselves as parents, almost without realizing it, they see themselves in the setting of a large and giving family. If they are an isolated couple living in an impersonal crowded city or in a sprawling suburb they have just recently moved to, they will have nobody to call on to help take care of a child. Such couples—and also other couples who have more grounds for thinking they may get the help of an extended family—had better check as soon as possible with the extended family on whether help is going to be available, and how much. Some couples need relatives' help with the first child, some need it with later children, some seem to need it all their lives. Whenever it is going to be needed, it is important for everyone involved to be open and clear about the real situation.

IMPLICATIONS OF FAMILY SIZE

How many children people should have may be debated both in terms of personal preference and as an issue facing all societies because of the dangers of overpopulation. The chances are that if most people chose how many children they really and truly desired and had only that many children, there would still be great diversity in family sizes. On the other hand, in cultures where people have generally greater expectations for happiness and fulfillment, parents consider each child as special and important and therefore tend to have fewer children, since they expect to provide more for each one. The right number of children for any couple is the number they can welcome into the family as potential sources of joy and happiness, and raise happily and contentedly, without anyone's life being distorted by unfulfilled needs. Such families seldom have a great many children.

In our society some advocate just one child per couple. With an only child, they point out, parents get to know their child very well, and their relationship can be intense, rewardingly so. They point out that the parents can devote more of their energies and resources to the development of just one child. They also say it is morbid to focus on the possibility that the child may die since, today, most children do grow to adulthood and outlive their parents. They emphasize that having one child allows mother, father, and child to have fuller lives with more time to pursue their individual interests and pleasures.

People who are against only one child in a family say that an only child runs a high risk of growing up self-centered, greedy, and insecure. The parents' hopes and frustrations and neuroses focus on this one child, and the burden on her or him to be all that the parents wish him or her to be is frequently overwhelming. If disaster strikes and the child dies, the parents, having invested in her or him all their aspirations for the joy and fulfillment children can bring, are likely to be so seriously bereaved that they will not recover from the psychological stress of this tragedy. Some who are against the one-child family also point out that if many couples had only one child, the population decrease would be so rapid as to create social and economic havoc.

The two-child family has many advantages. It gives people the chance to become parents more than once, and two children offer greater security against the risk of death. People who have two children also have a chance at having one of each sex. Two children make for greater diversity in the family; there are two human beings growing, developing, acquiring friends, interests, and points of view. This size family is not likely to become an overwhelming burden. There are two children, and two parents to take care of them. Each of the children has a sibling. Each has the chance to grow up with another child to learn to share with and cope with another person. Having a sibling tends to minimize the danger that a child will acquire an exaggerated picture of his or her own importance and thus, be unwilling to accept other people's needs, desires, even rights. Having a sibling tends to give a child the opportunity to learn to cope with success and failure at an early stage in life—being the victorious one, the successful one, the one who accomplishes something one day, and the vanquished one, the one who fails, the one who doesn't achieve anything the next.

All these happy possibilities do not automatically become real, however. Parents are not relieved of any of the complicated duties of raising children by having any particular number. Still, many of the young couples who are today making a definite decision on family size are choosing two children. They see the potential advantages listed above, and they see another one. Many women today don't want to become pregnant again and again. Rather, they want to have their children and then go on to other experiences. Frequently they want to take a job and give the family two incomes.

In the past, having a large family was often a deliberate choice, since it had many great advantages. Child mortality was extremely high, so families needed several children to ensure that at least some of them would grow to adulthood. Children were the only possible insurance most parents had against becoming destitute and uncared for in their old age. This was not always great insurance, but many people tried to provide for their old age that way. Particularly in rural communities, children were a great economic asset to their families. As they grew, they became the labor force of the family.

Most of this has changed for most people. In the United States, child mortality is low. Parents have an excellent chance of raising all their children to adulthood. Parents also usually have the whole responsibility for taking care of them in infancy and childhood, watching over their development, and providing for their financial needs. This includes paying for part or all of their education, which can be expensive and indeed, can last well into the childrens' adulthood. Times have changed from the days when many children were expected to contribute to their own upkeep as soon as size and physical strength allowed. The education and training necessary to prepare a child for our complex world can take many, many years, placing a tremendous burden on the parents. And finally, our elderly are increasingly being supported by governmental agencies and pension plans, rather than by their own children.

In various ways all these factors mitigate against having a large family. Nonetheless there are today, and will always be, people who intensely desire to raise large families, who feel that they will not be fulfilled as human beings unless they do. For some of them this will be the right and healthy choice. There are champions in all areas of endeavor, including champion parents, couples who will be happy and do a good job parenting a large number of children. But if people want several children—because they find little children adorable or bigger children fascinating, or because they think they're going to feel successful and loved, secure and powerful when surrounded by a lot of children—for them to have several children may work out well as long as they are willing and able to pay the price for fulfilling their fantasies.

To sum up, for all parents it is important to have only the number of children they can comfortably raise. Too many children can become a serious stress on the marriage. The way to arrive at the right number is, as in other major decisions, through introspection, self-evaluation, and a thorough appraisal of outside reality.

IMPLICATIONS OF BOYS OR GIRLS

Can the sex of the children become a stress on the marriage? Realistically, no, but for certain people, because of their psychological makeup, yes. A person's feelings about any given situation can make it advantageous or disadvantageous. There are parents who do not enjoy raising sons and parents who find raising daughters a tremendous burden. Nothing absolute makes boys more difficult or easier to raise than girls. Whether boys are easier to raise than daughters, or vice versa, is not due to some inevitable, unalterable qualities in either sex. Rather, it is due to the human nature of the particular parents or children involved. Some parents find little boys charming and adolescent boys difficult, or little boys difficult and adolescent boys charming; likewise, some find little girls sweet and adolescent girls impossible, or little girls whiny and adolescent girls delightful. These parents have difficulties with behavior typically exhibited at particular developmental stages, some pattern that reawakens certain of the parent's own unconscious conflicts and difficulties which were never resolved to his or her satisfaction. For example, one father wanted to be popular with the girls as an adolescent but wasn't. His teenage son is handsome and very popular. It would be pleasant for the father if he could be proud and enjoy his son's success but, in fact, he's jealous. He doesn't know it, but that's why he gets very angry over small matters like the son's coming home half an hour late from a date.

Prospective parents sometimes desire either a boy or girl so strongly as to experience disappointment, deprivation, even a sense of failure when a child of the desired sex does not come their way. Their strong feelings are based on the usually unconscious symbolic significance that male or female children have for them. Usually without being aware of it, they want a boy or a girl in order to fulfill some deep unrealistic personal desire. For instance, some people who have always been dissatisfied with themselves, dream of creating themselves as they wish they had been; some people who would have liked to be members of the other sex wish to recreate themselves as such; through children of their own sex, some people hope somehow to regain some lost opportunity or undo some important mistakes they feel they or their own parents made. Besides simply being miserable when they don't have a child of the right sex, these parents may even find it difficult to accept the child at all, so that an unhealthy, disturbed relationship is the result, producing destructive behavior toward this child, such as rejection, overprotection, competition, or seduction.

In relation to other attributes too, parents may have preconceived ideas about what kind of children they desire or deserve–intellectual or athletic, quiet or boisterous, slender or plump–and so increase the chances that having children will become stressful. For again, if their children turn out to be different from the preconceived model, these parents will respond to them badly; the parents will be disappointed and find their children undesirable.

It's true, of course, that all parents-to-be have feelings about what they want their children to be like. But most parents have their children, accept them with love, and enjoy them–whether they are the "right" or "wrong" sex, whether they're bookish or athletic, whether they're thin or fat. Parents who can't do this have distorted their desires into blueprints of the children they want. The outlook can't be happy for their children, whether they're the "right" or "wrong" kind. Too much is expected of them. No one wants to live out anyone else's blueprint for a life.

Technology is beginning to make it possible for people to determine the sex of a child before it's born. Amniocentesis, besides revealing genetic defects, indicates the sex of a fetus. If the sex is undesirable, the pregnancy can be aborted, so that the couple can try again until the test indicates the desired sex. The abortion is a substantial physical shock to the mother, since amniocentesis cannot be performed before the fetus is about sixteen weeks old, and it usually takes another two or three weeks for the cells obtained to be grown so their sex can be determined. My clinical experience suggests that a couple who will do this to have a child of the sex they want, does not have the maturity to be good parents. They regard a child as an object, not as a flesh-and-blood human being, and they won't be able to deal with the many unpredictable factors involved in raising a child. A child's development is influenced by many circumstances beyond the control of even the most thoughtful and aware parents. Even if sex is determined and chosen, the parents still have no guarantee about what kind of boy or girl they will have. Parents who go to such extremes to choose the sex of a child will have trouble coping with these truths.

FAMILY LIFE WITHOUT CHILDREN

Even though having a child is a demanding, time-consuming, and long-lasting commitment, for most people today it does not stretch out through most of adult life. With increased life expectancy and a decreasing number of children in families, most couples do not spend the major part of their married life raising or even living with their children. Many couples spend some years together before they have children, and can look forward to many years together after they have finished raising them. Some couples, of course, choose to live their whole married life alone together by deliberately choosing not to have children.

There are no societies or people for whom the issue of whether to have children is completely unimportant. All cultures award children a special place. Even in cultures or subcultures where they are used as cheap labor, some special provision is made for their survival and safety. Because of the importance that children have, a couple's decision not to have children always has great personal implications as well as social ones.

Childlessness can be stressful regardless of whether it is a deliberate choice or a biological circumstance. Strife will arise in a marriage when one of the partners is not willing to have children while the other wants them. If basic agreement is possible, the couple still need to work out their feelings about not having children together.

They will have to consider the following things: children make great physical, emotional, and financial demands. Some couples feel they will be closer without children because they won't have these demands and distractions. Some feel their sex life will be more intense, for instance, because they will not lack privacy, or be physically tired. What will fill their lives instead of children?—perhaps more time and money to spend on their home, clothing, travel, hobbies, books, records, going to the theater, fishing, hunting, tennis. Some people would rather spend their adult lives in the company of other adults, pursuing adult activities, because they believe that doing so will make them happier and intensify their marital bond.

Whether all or any of these alternatives will make particular people, male or female, happier is too much an individual matter to generalize. The better a couple can evaluate their strengths, energies, feelings about each other, and what they want out of their married life, the clearer their choice will be. People who choose not to have children after an honest evaluation of their needs and limitations are more likely to be making a reasonable choice with which they can live, than are people who choose to have children without carefully estimating their own capabilities.

Cynthia and Gene, for example, are childless, although not by choice. They were students together, and had the same views on social issues, religion, even how to spend money. They agreed on music, on the people they liked and disliked, on sports. They seldom became locked in petty jealousies and, in general, were supportive of each other's work efforts. During the fifth year of their marriage, they decided they were ready for children, and were surprised when Cynthia did not conceive after six months of trying. When they found that Gene's sperm count was extremely low, they were shocked and deeply disappointed. However, they will probably continue to be a successful couple, whether they decide to stay childless or to have a child by artificial insemination or adoption, because their marriage is based on mutual love, sexual appeal, trust, support, and understanding.

Sam and Fay, on the other hand, who are also childless, may not do as well. They have a teasing, competitive relationship in all areas, including sex. They compete about who is better during a particular sexual activity, who is more adventurous, who is less inhibited, who has more stamina, who has more endurance, who can do it longer, better, more often. They compete about who makes more money, who has a harder job, whose job is more important, who is more productive, who has a more brilliant career ahead. Their competition is so intense that they cannot be supportive or even accepting of each other, and have to go outside the marriage to find affection and acceptance. Fay is very close to her sister, and Sam to his father; and friends are enormously important to them both. However, they don't keep their friends long, because they impose such exorbitant demands on them, using the friendships for the support and nurturance that should come from the marriage.

After four years of marriage they decided to start a family, but with no success. They found that Sam's sperm count was extremely low, and they're having much difficulty dealing with their childlessness. It's been a blow to Sam to find out he's at fault since it makes him feel inferior. It's hard for Fay to be supportive because she always wants him to be perfect so that she can show him off. His imperfection makes her feel inferior. It seems on the surface that they ought to be able to handle this problem; they're intelligent, educated, and they like their jobs. But they are also very controlling, manipulative people, and so they're likely to have great difficulty coping with their imposed childlessness.

To make childlessness a successful choice, people must be able to handle its consequences to their own satisfaction. They will be members of a minority group, since most married adults still choose to have children. Their life styles and interests will be affected by their choice. Activities that are of great importance and interest to most married adults will not concern them. They won't have the variety of interests that children develop and then share with their parents. They will also not be able to experience the intense love and devotion children have for parents—that exuberant, demonstrative, physical show of affection. It is a most special experience to be loved by one's own little child. As children grow older, the relationship with the parents becomes more complicated, and usually some conflicts develop in it. But throughout life, people tend to retain a strong element of love for their parents, and the feelings of parents toward their offspring are truly intense. People who elect not to have children deprive themselves of this particular experience; they have fewer people who love them intensely, and also fewer people on whom to lavish love and attention.

A couple should discuss the whole issue of children before they marry to establish whether they both are interested in having children. That way they avoid the possibly traumatic discovery after marriage that one is determined to have children and the other one hates the idea. Infertility, on the other hand, most often is not discovered until after marriage. With modern medical methods many couples of low fertility can be helped to conceive and produce children, but this often requires a substantial amount of trying. So far, medical science does not have good tests for fertility except in cases of gross anatomical disorders. In other cases, the only foolproof test of fertility is the birth of a child. So the issue of a couple's possibly being unable to produce children usually arises only after they have been trying to have a child for some time. Infertility usually is caused by one partner; very rarely are both infertile.

The discovery by people who hope and expect to have children that they are going to be barren brings real and strong stress into their marriage. Some people experience this as a disaster. The way a couple will handle the stress will depend on their strength and resilience in the face of misfortune and their ability to handle it together. For some couples, having to face the fact that one of the partners is sterile will be so serious a blow that the marriage will deteriorate and perhaps dissolve.

People who have strong, positive feelings for one another can stay together and cope with this stress by compensation. They may indulge themselves more. They can feel freer to allot their resources as they wish, and they can travel or pursue hobbies. To compensate for the lack of relationships with children, they may develop strong ties to other adults or commit themselves to a service organization and do altruistic work. In other words, they develop the same options as deliberately childless couples. In the process their love and devotion to one another, built on thorough knowledge of one another and much time together, can become very strong.

Childless couples who did not want to be childless do not have to spend their lives entirely without children. They can and do become devoted aunts and uncles and favorite neighbors, or they can volunteer for service work with children. Some take in foster children. Childless couples who want more than this have two other options. One is artifical insemination, which can be undertaken if the infertility problem is in the male. The second is adoption.

Artificial insemination is quite common, and it can work out well, but it is a very special way to solve infertility. The couple must think through and be able to handle the implications of conceiving a child in this way and then later raising it. The child is theirs but not quite theirs. If it turns out to be a difficult child, emotional problems may arise that will be hard to handle. For instance, the husband may blame the real father's genes, and the mother may then blame her husband for not having been able to impregnate her.

Legal adoption of someone else's child can be a very successful solution to infertility, but it also demands deep and deliberate thought. An adopted child can cause stress in the marriage in all the same ways that a biological child can, if the parents do not understand or are not ready for the commitment of parenthood. There are also special stresses of adoption. Adoption must be honestly and openly acknowledged and accepted. Couples should not adopt children and then pretend that it's the same thing as the birth of their own child. There is no need to advertise the fact to the world at large, but for adoption to be a family secret is not healthy. More crucial, though, are the adoptive parents' feelings. Adopting a child cannot be just like having a biological child. You must ask yourself the question of whether your feelings for the child are as strong as your feelings would have been for your own offspring, and come to terms with any pain the answer might give. You must also help the adoptees to cope with their own painful feelings about being adopted. If these matters go unresolved, they are likely to cause stress. Other problems may arise if one or both parents have rigid ideas about what kind of child they want and are unable to accept the child they actually adopted. Although this may also happen to biological parents who are disappointed by their own children, the problem is apt to be more severe with adoptees, because without even being aware of it, many parents expect adopted children, having been chosen, to be very special, even ideal.

Formal, legal adoption of totally unrelated people is a modern phenomenon. Today, because of improved contraception and legalization of abortion, the number of children available for adoption has decreased, and the kind of children available for adoption has changed. This means that couples who want to adopt children, and specifically the kind of children they had hoped to have themselves, are finding that there are far fewer children available for adoption. Some want children so much that they are willing, even eager, to adopt children from a different racial background, or children with handicaps. Those who undertake such a commitment need to understand and be able to cope with its special demands. The more different the child from the parents, the greater the demands on them will be.

In recent years, an increasing number of people who already have biological children have also adopted children as their own contribution toward a better world. Such adoptions, although undertaken with the best intentions and the most noble motives, may have troublesome and complicated consequences, especially if the adoptees are from a different background. This should only be undertaken by people who understand the practical and psychological problems of raising such a child.

HANDICAPPED CHILDREN

With reasonable care we can, for the most part today, expect to bring children through the illnesses of childhood to a healthy adulthood. Most of them, with good nutrition, rest, proper immunization against disease, and attention to safety, will suffer only limited periods of illness.

But when a child is seriously handicapped or does have a severe, long-lasting illness with permanent effects, or from which there will be no recovery, parents will experience extreme stress. Raising a chronically sick or handicapped child is more demanding than raising a healthy one. The child needs more care—in many cases specialized care over long periods of time. The child may be cut off from some of the community facilities that help in rearing children—schools, day camps, and so on—which are useless without special adjustments for the handicapped child. At home, much more effort will have to be spent to create a reasonable environment for a sick or handicapped child—more energy, more time, more money. All this extra care places a real burden on the marriage; in addition, of course, the intangible rewards of seeing a child grow and develop skills and independence are slower, often much slower, in coming.

Personal emotional difficulties are also the lot of every parent of a seriously sick child. These difficulties differ from parent to parent, depending on individual background and experience, and influence the way each parent and each couple copes with the problems they now face. Every parent has visions of an ideal child, and if the child from birth is seriously ill or later becomes so, any parent will experience great feelings of disappointment and sadness. These feelings sometimes make the emotional burden of having a sick child more difficult than the practical problems.

In addition, the more important a problem, the more likely we are to be plagued by our ambivalence, our mixed feelings. The illness of a child, whether it's due to congenital problems, disease, or injury after birth, tends to bring out the negative aspects of this ambivalence. A parent experiences doubts and regrets about previous actions and choices. Such feelings are likely to lead to blame, often intense blame, of self, of parents, of spouse and his or her relatives, of other people, of the past in general. The blame may accentuate any feelings of dislike that the marital partners have for one another. Then come feelings of guilt and shame for having all the other bad feelings. These confused emotions make it harder for parents of a sick or handicapped child to cope with a difficult reality, let alone support and reassure one another, as the situation demands.

Two case histories may be cited to show how a handicapped child can affect family life. Both children suffer from Down's syndrome. The first child, Billy, was born to Margie and Joe. Margie is and has always been tense and perfectionistic, and has trouble dealing with unexpected or difficult things. She reacts to criticism poorly and is terrified of failure. Joe also tends to be a perfectionist, and pays a great deal of attention to details. He tries to control his anxiety by overplanning. Margie was thirty and Joe was thirty-two when Billy, their only child, was born. They felt terrible disappointment when they found out he was handicapped, and responded to the problem, like most couples, with grief, frustration, anger, and depression. They have never really recovered from their depression. They are still trying to deal with Billy the way they have always dealt with other problems—by overcompensating, by trying to undo the damage through effort. They spend hours trying to compensate for Billy's slowness. They are convinced that if they only put in enough time and effort they'll be able to compensate for his limited capacity. Of course, their efforts are futile and lead to nothing but frustration for all three of them. Instead of learning to accept and deal with Billy for what he is and even enjoy his successes, they stubbornly refuse to give up their unrealistic efforts to change him. They do not plan to have another child, although they know that the chances of their having another baby like Billy are small, and they also know that amniocentesis would reveal the presence of the syndrome in the fetus. They would rather live with their unhappiness and make misguided and futile attempts to change Billy.

Andrea and Jim, who had this same tragedy happen to them, deal with it completely differently. They are basically energetic, happy people who don't feel any need for total control. They feel they can deal with whatever happens, and indeed they've been quite successful doing so. When their first child, who is normal, was three years old, Nathan was born. Nathan is afflicted with Down's syndrome. Andrea and Jim were stunned, grief-stricken, and unhappy, but they were able to talk about their sadness and disappointment, deal with their depression, and overcome it. They took Nathan home and tried to integrate him into their family. They were busy with their first boy and didn't spend an unusual amount of time with Nathan. They take good care of him, but don't push him, don't feel they have to overstimulate him. They accept their two children and deal with both of them realistically. The older boy receives intellectual stimulation and attention; Nathan is given care and simple, accepting love. When Nathan was four, Andrea gave birth to a third child, a healthy normal girl. Andrea and Jim enjoy and accept their three children. Yes, Nathan is a source of sorrow. They understand his limitations, and they are concerned about his future, but their life essentially moves along normally. They don't spend excessive amounts of time and energy on Nathan, although they use all community resources available for him. He goes to a special kindergarten where he receives speech therapy, but Andrea will not take him for extra speech therapy because it would take too much time away from the other children. She also wants to be able to take the oldest boy to Boy Scouts and to have time to play with her little girl.

The stress that a sick child places on a marriage thus often tests the marriage and the devotion of the partners to one another. A marginal marriage, a marriage where people have little commitment to one another and are mainly looking out for their immediate gratification, is not likely to withstand much of this kind of stress and is likely to collapse. A more stable marriage is more likely to stand up. Even in a good marriage, of course, the stress that arises from the special pain of a sick child is draining; the partners need support and sustenance from one another in bearing their burden, which is not merely a long-term problem, but also a daily one. Frequently, however, they both feel unhappy—and so may not be able to support and sustain one another enough. Families with chronically ill children have more conflict and discord. Specialized professional help in dealing with the painful emotions can be very useful.

The death of a child, however, often is less of a burden on such a great loss entails—and, again, emotional complications. Grief culminates in mourning. Mourning is complicated by the presence not only of realistic feeings of loss, but also of unrealistic feelings of guilt or blame or both. If there is blame, there are likely to be recriminations. How could it have been prevented? Who could have prevented it? At a deeper level, any negative feelings that relate to this child that either parent may have will cause problems between them. For instance, if one of the parents entered the marriage mainly for the purpose of having children, when a child dies, that parent may feel betrayed, and the other parent may be made desperate.

The death of a child however, often is less of a burden on a marriage than is living with a seriously ill child. The death of a child is a one-time, major disaster, through which the couple has to help one another so they can go on together; they may already have another child or children, or can have them in the future, but the burden of a seriously ill or handicapped child is constant, and it often produces a pervading hopelessness in the couple's life.

CHAPTER 5

The Practical Side of Marriage

WORK

We begin to approach the world of work in childhood, with the chores and lessons that prepare us for adult functioning. For most of us, work is a major part of life, and any condition that enhances our chances for success at work enhances our chances for happiness. Marriage is one such condition. Relieved from sexual pressure and with the security of having a loved person with whom to pool resources, married people find that they can devote more time and energy to work than they could as single people.

During stressful periods in marriage one or both people may experience difficulty in meeting their work commitments to the full, because they are spending a great deal of their energy on their problems. They become too preoccupied and torn to be able to be very productive at work; but this is not because they're married, it's because they have problems.

Young people are sometimes urged not to get married until they have gone some way in their careers, as if marriage were detrimental to career progress. Again the problem isn't marriage as such, but rather that when youngsters are immature, the marital situation becomes distracting. Marriage is conducive to pursuing one's work, provided work is a priority. At certain times priorities shift. For instance, a couple with young children may choose to devote a lot of time to them instead of to career advancement.

Another advantage married people have is their greater financial security. Married people tend to be in a better financial position, by and large, than do single people of the same age and general social status. Married people seem to have both higher financial standing today and greater security for tommorrow—for instance, greater protection against adverse circumstances with more life, health, and fire insurance than single people.

As I have already said, marriage fulfills people's needs for sex and a close human relationship, freeing their time and energy for work. In a marriage that is going well, a person lives with a spouse, and usually also with children, in an atmosphere of caring and being cared about. This kind of involvement tends to make him or her more optimistic, more interested in the future, and more deeply invested in trying to ensure future stability. Optimism and interest in the future help in reaching financial success. A happily married person has a partner interested in the same long-term goals; they have combined physical, mental, and financial resources that they use to spur each other on during good times, and, very importantly, to support each other during bad times.

Work-related problems can of course create stress in a marriage. One of the more difficult problems has to do with having made a poor career choice. Your choice of what you do to earn a living is not, of course, an entirely free choice. It's a compromise between what is available to you and what your abilities and limitations will allow. When careers are poorly matched to people's talents and skills, they become anxious. They dread the daily routine, they fear losing their job, they fear financial loss. Working under these conditions makes them unhappy—they can neither hope nor expect that their stressful work situation will get any better, and this daily unhappiness puts a stress on their marriage.

Any seriously draining work is like a slow poison in the

worker's life. Work that is too demanding physically can leave him or her no strength to take care of the house, to make love, to play with the children, to maintain friendships, to be a host or hostess, to be a guest. A work environment that is always frenetic and tense can mean that the worker comes home without the psychic energy to be interested in what the rest of the family did all day, what the family problems are, or what is going on in the world at large. It seems too much to read a book or watch a movie on TV or even leaf through a magazine. Work that demands excessive hours leaves no time to do anything else—to be sexually active, let alone sexually imaginative—to be with the children, keep up other relationships with family or friends, help with the dishes or do the laundry, take care of the garden, hang a picture, or go shopping. Work that demands long absences from home puts a burden on spouse and children. Work can demand that people spend many hours beyond working hours studying, learning, polishing the skills necessary to keep their work at top level, with the same kind of effect on a family. Like people's physical and psychological energies, time is a precious commodity, and work should not be allowed to take up too much of it if there is any way to avoid it.

Attitudes about work and work-related matters, as well as work itself, may also be stressful, especially for people who do not enjoy the process of work, but live only for the moment of achievement. They are in for a lot of dissatisfaction and disappointment. Sometimes anticipated moments of achievement never come, and even if they do, it is only after and between much boring but necessary activity. If people enjoy work before, during, and after the moment of achievement—if they enjoy the routine, the process, the striving—they will be happier. People who enjoy only achievement itself tend to have unhappy lives and marriages. Their rewards are sporadic and momentary, and the pressure they feel to get that momentary applause, that extra medal at the end, demands an extraordinary wearing effort.

As for wanting success, that ambition too can cause marital problems. Success in any job or career is uncertain, and only a small number of people ever achieve positions of leadership in any field. Although most people would like to achieve success, when the desire for success knows no bounds, it can dominate lives and marriages. One spouse may have great needs for tangible rewards or prestige, or both, and attempt to gain them by exploiting or using the partner. Women do this to men, and men do this to women. Marriages like this have the potential for disaster.

Take Alice and Harry's marriage, for example. She is a doctor's daughter, her two brothers are doctors, and Harry is also a physician. Alice grew up in a beautiful house in a lovely suburb where her father was a prominent citizen. When Alice and Harry married, she was a kindergarten teacher, and he was a resident in internal medicine. Alice felt safe and special then and wants to make sure her security continues.

Alice is an ambitious woman; her ambition is directed toward making absolutely certain that Harry is as successful as she wants him to be. Shortly after they married she stopped teaching, and has since devoted herself full-time to being a wife and mother, which to Alice means that she oversees her husband's and children's work, habits, achievements, and successes. Alice is fortunate because her husband is both capable and successful; so are her children, but nonethless Alice watches them all constantly. Nothing they achieve is enough for her, and she is always working to help them. She joins clubs to help build her husband's practice, and enlarge his image in the community. She encourages, cajoles, and exhorts him to get on hospital and medical committees. She wants him to be active in local politics and sit on the board of the country club. She tries to make sure that he reads his professional journals and, like a nagging mother, quizzes him about it. Every professional achievement, every professional honor that he receives, she feels is equally hers. He is her trophy getter, and she sees that he stays healthy by supervising his diet, his exercise, and, of course, his finances. She is blind to the fact that her bossiness creates anger and hostility in him toward her, stresses their relationship, and decreases his tenderness for her. It's hard to love a dictator even if she is your own wife.

Frank, like Alice, uses his spouse to get what he wants. He's a salesman, well suited for his job, but what he wants is way above what he can afford. He is always telling his wife, Beatrice, how vital it is to both of them that he have flashy clothing and a big car, and maybe a boat. They should also go out a lot to help his career. Frank insists that Beatrice must work and make money. She doesn't mind working, but she doesn't want to leave their two-year-old son with babysitters six days a week. Frank ignores her arguments, and Beatrice is beginning to feel she may have to choose between her husband and her son.

There are marriages that are entered into for pragmatic reasons. They can suceed if both people understand clearly what they want, if they both agree to the arrangement, and if they are willing to forego other things that may be inconsistent. Typically, one spouse must want to be married to someone whose appeal and desirability largely stem from a great willingness and drive to achieve success in the world. This spouse must not suddenly change after the marriage and demand a great deal more, so that the other one feels used and unloved.

People who actually desire a spouse who will provide improved social status and impressive material wealth often choose a spouse on the more culturally approved basis of sexual attractiveness or emotional appeal. Then, once married, they start to demand great achievement and success. Sometimes, indeed, job achievement becomes the only acceptable sign of love and devotion. One partner thus constantly demands new achievements from the other to fulfill grandiose personal wishes, without paying any attention to the other's actual inclinations and abilities.

One example of a couple in which one married for pragmatic reasons and the other for sexual attraction is Donna's marriage to Byron.

She is beautiful, and Byron was her boss before they were married. He was a bachelor in his forties and not especially handsome—short, with scars of severe acne. As an adolescent he was shy and awkward, but very intelligent; he decided then he would compensate for his lack of good looks by becoming successful and cultured. Donna is from a small town; after high school she went to secretarial school and moved to the city. She was pretty and fun to be with, so she was taken to the theater, to movies, to good restaurants. When her boss, Byron, asked her out, she was pleased and flattered. When he asked her to marry him she accepted. Byron was not her ideal Prince Charming, and Byron, too, was aware that he was twenty years older than she, and that it was his success that had given him a young and beautiful wife. Both are honest and good. Both appreciate what they are getting, and their marriage can succeed as long as they don't demand, after the marriage, the things that they did not ask for before.

It is much more honest, realistic, and conducive to happiness for people who know they want to reach the top of the ladder, to say so from the start; or, better, to get into the race and climb the ladder themselves rather than putting the burden on their spouse. Some people who want success find it hard to be this honest; some even find it difficult to appraise their own talents and limitations.

Again, the issue is complex. If you define an attractive and sexually stimulating partner as someone with great vigor, ambition, and ability, it is certainly appropriate for you to look for such a person to marry. But you can't know ahead of time whether you're marrying just a scientist or a future Nobel Laureate, just an actor or a potential star; and you shouldn't worry about it. What you can legitimately do is realistically judge a potential spouse's energies, ambitions, and talents, because these things will be relevant to the life you will lead when you've married him or her.

Take Gloria and Bruce, for instance. Their parents were friends, and their backgrounds were alike. They grew up in affluent homes; their parents told them they were right for each other and that they should marry, which they did. Bruce now has a job in his father's successful business, and he and Gloria still get expensive gifts from both sets of parents. Bruce and Gloria expect and are used to having the very best, better than most other people. Now that they are married, they are beginning to wonder if each of them chose the best possible person, and if the marriage is perhaps not the very best—that is, is it really all they deserve and expect. Each is thinking about how to change the other into the very best person for themselves because neither is used to compromise or accommodation. Both think they deserve and can get everything they want, and each is unaware that a spouse is not an object and trying to change a spouse creates resentment and hostility.

In general, it is not the particular job or career that causes stress in a marriage, but the way individuals deal with it. Married scholars and carpenters, postal clerks and merchants, astronauts and politicians, psychiatrists and obstetricians may each be happy at work or be miserable. Nor is work division between husband and wife stressful per se, whether both spouses work outside the home, or only the man works outside the home, or only the woman works outside the home. In each group some people are content with their achievements at work, and others are not.

Alfred and Dinah, for instance, are examples of people who are never satisfied. They have been able to buy a house in a neighborhood where most of their neighbors are more affluent than they, and instead of being pleased that they've been successful enough to have such a nice house at their early age, they pressure themselves to keep up with their neighbors' cars, clothes, furniture, and vacations. They talk only about promotions, office politics, how they're pushing themselves by taking courses, impressing their bosses, and maneuvering at the office to get ahead. Their marriage is structured around these unrealistic ambitions, for neither one will ever achieve enough.

Work becomes a stress on a marriage when one spouse cannot accept something about the other's work—style, commitment, tensions, pressures, or whatever—and demands that the work be given up or somehow drastically changed. Work wlll also invariably cause problems if one marital partner refuses to accept the necessity to work, except, of course, in wealthy marriages. However, most people, men and women, need to contribute somehow to the financial arrangement that supports their marriage, and it's a practical and psychological burden when a spouse refuses to participate in this very basic adult activity. A central part of being an adult is to be productive and provide for oneself and any other people one assumes responsibility for, like a mate and children. Any marriage in which the spouses refuse to make peace with this reality generally will not survive.

As an example, take Bryan's marriage. He's a construction worker, and a union official. However, even this position does not guranatee that he works all the time, and he is often laid off for weeks on end. He and Irma have two children, and because of Bryan's situation, she has to work. She has a full-time office job and is, at times, the main breadwinner of the family. Bryan resents that. He insists that she do all the household work when she comes home, while he watches TV, reads the paper, and drinks beer. He doesn't mind if the children help out, but he won't. When he's out of work for more than a few days he becomes quite difficult. He makes fun of her work and of her friends, and won't talk about whatever problems she may have at the office. The longer he's not working, the more he demands from her sexually, and the less he does around the house. He will make absolutely no effort to find any other kind of job, and when Irma asks him to find some way to supplement their income, he says she's attacking his manhood. Irma is beginning to find the situation intolerable.

A couple's careers should provide them with a satisfying standard of living. A fair and equitable effort should be made by both partners, and each should agree that both of them are doing what's fair. When one partner feels taken advantage of and used by the other, it will cause a great deal of resentment.

People do differ, of course, in their capacity and their productivity. Some people can work longer hours. Some can produce more than others in a given amount of time without feeling harried. It is conducive to a stress-free married life for married people to realize and accept the fact that enormous individual differences exist in the quantity, quality, and variety of work that the spouses can handle. Neither one should demand performances from themselves or their partners that are beyond their capabilities. If you can't accept your own or your spouse's limitations in the area of work, your marriage will have tremendous problems. Of course we should try to achieve all that we can, be as successful as possible, gain as many of the desirable rewards of a productive adult life as are available to us. But it's unrealistic not to be able to be satisfied at all unless conditions are perfect, and you have just what you want and what you think you deserve. Some circumstances are not controllable.

Excessive devotion to work can also stress a marriage. A job may be too demanding; but so may dedication to a vocational goal, such that a career is the major pursuit of life, and little time, energy, or desire is left for anything else. The work may be fascinating and worthwhile but if it entirely consumes the worker, his or her marriage will suffer. Fatigue makes people less resilient. It weakens their defenses, and emotional problems that people can keep under control when they feel healthy, relaxed, and refreshed, become prominent. Tired people are much more likely to be demanding, irritable, suspicious, insecure, supersensitive, quarrelsome—in general, difficult to live with. Such behavior will stress their marriages.

Gregory, for instance, is unreasonably devoted to work. He came from a broken home, where he received very little attention. His father abandoned the family, and the mother had to support the family as best she could with very marginal skills. Although Gregory showed some technical talent in high school, no one encouraged him. He got a job with a company that made computers, and became fascinated by them. He began to spend his lunch hours watching the programmers and learning from them. He took advantage of company in-service training and was soon promoted. He began to take courses on his own time. In his work, Gregory has found something to heal the hurts and neglects of his childhood. But, although he has found a realistic and rational outlet for his natural talent, his fascination is also being fueled by unconscious hurts and unconscious misconceptions. Consequently his behavior is only partly rational. He is always engrossed in one computer magazine or another. He stays late at work. He takes courses. He completely neglects his young wife and baby. He is essentially deserting his family as his father did. He puts himself and his time into his work, so that there is very little left over for his family.

Faith is someone else who is so drained by her work that it's having a bad effect on her marriage. She was the youngest of four children and the only girl. Although she was much loved, she always felt that somehow she was not as good as her brothers. They loved her and played with her, but she felt more like a toy than a person. She did her best to keep up with them, and was considered quite a tomboy. She was a good student at school, did well in math and science, and became an engineer. She married a colleague who is also an engineer.

Faith knows she's competitive, but isn't aware how competitive she is with her husband. She works extremely hard, takes graduate courses after work, drives herself relentlessly. She complains that much of the glow is gone from her marriage. She feels sad and disheartened about it. Their sex life is not what it used to be. She somehow doesn't have much interest in it, and finds it difficult to get involved. She is surprised that this has happened to them. They were strongly attracted to one another, and their ideas about marriage were much the same. Faith is convinced that there's some flaw in their relationship, and is considering sex therapy. She does not see that because of unconscious reasons she has a deep-seated need to excel in her work and to compete; and that she so exhausts herself by her work that she has no energy for anything else. Faith needs to realize that she's still trying to prove to her father and brothers that girls are as good as boys.

A marriage in which both partners do productive outside work that they find interesting and worthwhile has many advantages. Both make money; both understand what a daily work routine is like; both are likely to understand how much energy each has for activities that have nothing to do with work. On the other hand, if they both overwork, and they are tense and tired, their life together will lose vibrance and flavor, and their home can become an extremely grim place.

Differences in temperament, stamina, ability to withstand stress, and recuperative powers, particularly as related to work, often cause tension. What constitutes a correct amount of devotion to work is a personal assessment, and depends to a great degree on how successful each one is at work, in terms of both real rewards and subjective feelings.

Some people who are excessively devoted to work may be using it to solve their personal problems. They work too many hours, and the job is so important that there ceases to be any realistic ratio between the amount of work and the rewards—whether money, praise, recognition, power, or security. These overworkers are usually unaware that they are trying to solve a problem. They find realistic reasons for their behavior, and they remain blind to its consequences.

Sometimes they are avoiding facing their problem, as when they work long hours so they will not have to go home to a marriage and marital commitment they find difficult. Frequently their motivation is subtler: they are using work to raise their self-esteem in areas where they are afraid and less successful than at work. Certainly when people are successful in their work, they do feel better about themselves, and may actually become physically more attractive, intellectually more invigorated, and sexually more vigorous. Success stimulates and liberates energy. But, when people are afraid to face limitations in other areas and try to substitute success in work for becoming involved in the other areas, they are usually disappointed. They may tell themselves that work success will somehow spill over into those other areas and make everything all right. "If I make more money, the children will be easy to raise." "If I get that new position, we'll automatically have lots of friends." It doesn't happen. The children don't stop having problems. The couple is still lonely. Then there is the double stress of overwork plus frustration.

Because such excessive devotion to work is fueled by unconscious reasons, it is hard for a spouse to understand why his or her partner has to work so hard all the time. Lack of understanding gives rise to jealousy, resentment, and recrimination. The partner who is less devoted to work sees the other's work as a rival and feels belittled and insulted by it, so that it becomes much harder to give the overworker support.

One solution that is often tried is for both to go out to work, so that there will be less time for tension. This arrangement is not likely to help, because what it means is that there are two people whose work is not based in reality. It is often more helpful to realize that heavy work involvement may have an unconscious aspect, so that the spouse need not take it personally as long as it is not actually damaging. If the situation becomes overwhelming, professional help may be a good idea.

MALE AND FEMALE ROLES IN MARRIAGE

In our culture there are no married roles that men should always assume and none that women should always assume. There are no role arrangements that are beneficial or detrimental per se to a marriage. It does not matter in a marriage who earns the money, or more money, or who has a longer, more impressive job title. It makes no difference who does the laundry, who takes out the garbage, who cuts the lawn, who cooks the dinner, who does it sometimes, who does it most of the time. It doesn't matter who reads bedtime stories to the children or who diapers the children. So far, there is only one function that is absolutely and indubitably female. Only women can give birth, and then give their milk, to children, although some infants get most of all of theirs from specially prepared milk products and drink it from bottles. And so far, only males can contribute the sperm that produce children. Other functions are interchangeable, a matter of individual tastes, strengths, and abilities. There are traditionalists who will deny some of this, but this in essence is simply where our culture is today.

This has been liberating for many people, but before anyone gets carried away with praising our culture because it condones and encourages the flexible roles which are now fashionable or starts scorning those cultures which encourage roles we at the moment consider inequitable, archaic, and incorrect, it is important to be aware that the roles assumed by men and women in any culture are not arrived at strictly through intellectual or political processes. They are very much affected by economic factors and technological advances. The flexibility of marital roles in our culture would not be possible without advances in methods of contraception which have given us ways to get around our biological needs, and those advances were the result of advances in medicine and surgery, pharmacology, and indeed the rubber industry. This role flexibility also depends on our high standard of living, which has made possible a liberating level of education for more people than ever, plus wide ownership of the modern machines that perform with a great deal of success so many of the tasks of life and thereby increase the choices people are free to make.

It also is very, very important to be aware that what roles will be successful for a particular man or woman and their particular combination in marriage depend on their individual personalities and styles and priorities and, in the simplest terms, how they get along together. It is important that the roles they assume in their marriage be in harmony. Therefore there are no tricks in choosing a marital role or shortcuts to the correct role—no way to get around the need to evaluate oneself, to get to know one's partner as well as one can, and to do all one can from the start to build a lively and loving relationship with this particular spouse.

MONEY

Much has been written about the power of money, the evil of money, the glory of money, and, at a more mundane level, the necessity of having it. We all need money to be able to function and to maneuver; to be without it is to have diminished status.

Money becomes a stress on marriage when there is not enough of it—not enough to take care of real needs, or not as much as a couple feels they should have, or sometimes not as much as one partner feels they should have. Couples measure how much they should have in relation to their peers. They compare their financial standing with that of people of similar background, education, occupation, social status, age, and so on.

It is of course impossible to give a dollar figure for an income that will be adequate to prevent money from becoming a stress on a marriage. Even at low income levels there are great differences in how much or how little money people need in order to get along, and there is no level of society where everyone feels that all their stresses are attributable to the lack of money. Nor is there any level of society where everyone feels that they have enough money and that money plays no part in their stresses. Money can thus be a source of stress for a couple living on a small, medium, large, or even huge income.

Insufficient money in a marriage may be due to external factors beyond the control of either partner, such as an economic depression, illness, or the death of the breadwinner. A marriage may have financial problems that are brought about by the actions of one or both of the spouses. Whatever their cause, financial tensions may pose a particularly difficult burden for some married couples who are more stressed by circumstances that limit their financial resources than by almost any other kind of misfortune. Under financial pressure they are likely to turn on each other and blame one another for their money troubles—for not selling their stocks before the market fell, for not switching jobs before the job market got tight, even for not leaving the country before a war broke out.

Lillian, for example, places this kind of irrational blame on her spouse. Her father was a stockbroker; her parents' marriage was stormy, but it seemed to her that her father's financial success was what held them together, since he was always able to make life happy by buying her mother a new piece of jewelry, a fur coat, or an expensive vacation. Her parents also treated any problems Lillian had by buying her something new and expensive.

Lillian's first husband was a doctor, still young and therefore unable to support her in her unmarried style. Somehow his intelligence and dedication, and all the other qualities she admired before they were married grew meaningless, and she divorced him. Her second husband was a businessman, but his investments were not successful; although they had two children, she left him. Lillian's third husband is again not as financially successful as her father, and can't afford to give her the luxuries that she feels are necessary. They have begun to fight a lot.

There are variations in the way couples react to financial stress. Some will justify financial distress by blaming it on social circumstances that are also hurting their peers; these people find shared suffering easier to handle. Others, being more individualistic, prefer to blame themselves.

One way to make the matter of money stressful is to deny

the fact that you have to have it. As I have already said, some do this by simply refusing to work. Or, a spouse who has money may refuse to share it. The willingness to be responsible about money is most important to the well-being of a marriage; to refuse this responsibility or to carry it out minimally is detrimental in a tangible way. The irresponsibility of one marital partner is usually viewed by the other as a lack of commitment, concern, or even love, and sometimes this interpretation is correct. But here, as elsewhere, you should not project your own sense of what people should do into the situation. A mate may refuse to help financially because he or she has a great and unrecognizable fear of going out to work. There is no point trying to convince such a person that a good day's work is a totally natural thing, and then consider a refusal to be deliberate sabotage.

Christine is the wife of a man who has problems with work. Christine's parents were poor, and she's been working since high school. Her husband, Clement, went to college and became an engineer. They have two children, but to Christine it seems there are three, since she also has to take care of Clement's every need.

Clement is often angry. He complains about her selfishness, about how thoughtless and noisy and demanding the children are, how the neighbors are no good. He has many complicated physical ailments, but he doesn't like doctors because they don't know what they're talking about. His jobs have always been disasters. His boss is always demanding or tyrannical, his co-workers stupid and lazy. He never gets a break. Clement has quit many jobs.

Christine used to listen to his complaints, reassure him, tell him one day he'd find the right job. She used to wonder why he was so unlucky. Now she is beginning to suspect that maybe he's just lazy. The real trouble is that Clement is emotionally ill. He can't get along with people on the job, in the neighborhood, or at home because his emotional problems interfere with a realistic appraisal of the outside world. He sees other people as objects who have been placed there to take care of

Clement, because it is so hard for Clement to exist. They should be doing more to help him. His problems with work will only be solved when and if Clement is able to improve emotionally.

WORK AND MONEY

One partner may hold deep convictions about how money should be made and by whom—about where the money should come from. These beliefs sometimes derive much force from unconscious sources, and the spouse who holds them may have trouble adjusting to and coping with a situation that differs from his or her ideas about what is desirable or right.

Olga, for example, is married to a successful businessman, whom she loves. Their sex life, however, is only fair; she somehow always holds back, and can't get totally involved, although she doesn't know why. She does know that she's always finding fault with Walter, especially about what he does for a living. Although he's a prominent and honorable businessman, somehow that fact embarrasses her. Olga's father was a successful artist and her mother, although less successful, was a dancer. Her parents were very proud of their professions, their friends, and their life style, and they taught Olga that other ways of making a living might be necessary, but they were really only for those unfortunates who weren't artists. Olga was intelligent and capable, but she did not have any significant artistic talent. Her brother, who is a capable attorney, is also plagued by feelings of inadequacy and discontent.

Excessive devotion to money and a disproportionate allocation of time and energy to its acquisition can also cause much stress. Money partly derives its power and its desirability from its symbolic value, and some people attribute to it qualities that it does not possess, pursuing it for reasons that are neither sound nor realistic. In a word, they turn the pursuit of money into the worship of money.

People who spend every available minute making money rob themselves of the time to do the things money is supposed to enable one to do, and they also often endanger their health. Their marriages suffer, even when the money is being poured into the marriage. Goods and services may be present but, in human terms, so much else is missing.

Many cases in which this happens are like Bruno's. His father died when he was eleven years old.

Bruno's mother had to go out to work, the house was always cold and dirty, Bruno's mother cried and complained of being tired. They never went anywhere, nobody came to their house, they couldn't buy anything. All these things happened as Bruno saw it, because they had no money.

Bruno decided that money was the key to everything, and at fourteen he went to work, and life did seem better once he had money. Although Bruno never thought about it much he really didn't use his money because he was so busy with school and working. He thought he felt happier because he made money, but he actually felt happier because he felt more in control of his life. His pursuit of money gave him purpose, filled up his time, and made him feel in charge of himself.

Bruno now is married and has three children. He's generous to his wife and children, although he does get very nervous when they seem to spend too freely. He's particularly concerned that his children don't seem to know the value of money and don't seem to understand that it's necessary to work hard for money, but he leaves the children to his wife. She worries that he's a stranger to his children. Bruno explains that as long as he makes money and they have money, everything will be all right.

SPENDING MONEY

Spending money can also cause problems. The expenditure may be frugal or extravagant, but if it is not congruent with reality, it will cause trouble. It's a common misconception that money or things that it can buy will guarantee happiness. Money can't protect you from having to appraise yourself honestly enough to know what will and will not make you happy, though some people think it can. Among these people are many whose concentration on spending money comes out of some deep-seated, unconscious personal problem, which they need help to recognize. They continually spend, and they believe they are unhappy only because they have not yet bought enough or traveled enough, have not eaten in enough exotic places, don't have the right clothes, furniture, jewels, furs, books, records, coins, stamps, plants, cruises, tennis games.

People whose main occupation is to spend money are likely to have marital problems. To begin with, they are so involved in the activity of spending that they have very little time or energy left for anything else—including making the money to pay for what they buy. They spend household money on activities or objects that they and only they desire, and that even they often desire only for a moment or two. They give very little consideration to the way their behavior affects the other members of the family. Consequently everyone suffers because one person has a problem.

The outside world usually helps inflict the suffering. Money is the tool or vehicle of exchange, so that, how each of us handles it is very clear to other people, even strangers, and, more than we realize, it reveals our views and values. Certainly our friends see what we do with our money. Our culture does not approve of spendthrifts, people who "throw their money around," and this disapproval is expressed in many ways. Spendthrifts often are not able to pay for what they buy, which, among other things, may cause them—and their spouses—legal problems.

As a couple, both partners will have to deal with personal strife as well as these pressures from the real world. The spouse without the problem is very likely to try to change the other's point of view and actions, and if they're fortunate, will be able to do it. But more often, change doesn't occur, for two reasons. First, when an activity is all-consuming, it is fueled by unconscious forces highly resistant to suggestion, pleas, or even demands for change, so the two of them are very likely to fight about change. Second, one partner is apt to consider any advice, even good advice graciously given, as a reprimand and an attempt to take away pleasure and impose one will on the other.

Tony, for instance, in spite of all his wife can say, insists on spending his money in irrational ways. He came from a poor family, but went to school with the children of affluent and upwardly mobile parents, who had moved into his community. Tony did not do well at school; he felt left out and jealous of the life that his classmates lived. The thing that he most envied was that they had money. Right after high school Tony took a job; he works steadily with as much overtime as he can get, but he never has enough to pay the family bills. He spends too much money on the lottery, and on the horses. He bets all the time, but he's not particularly lucky. The more he loses gambling, the more he feels he has to keep on gambling to make up for his losses. He also likes new and shiny things. Photography was only a hobby of his for a very brief time but he has expensive photographic equipment that he's hardly ever used. He has fishing gear which he doesn't use either. The only hobby that holds his interest is gambling because he thinks that it can bring him what he saw his schoolmates have—easy money.

Money can also cause problems in the marriage in exactly the opposite way—when one partner is unwilling to part with money and hoards it. The only realistic use of money is to make life better. Given that some money should be kept in reserve for security against adversity, or saved toward some special goals, there is otherwise no virtue in just hoarding it. People who refuse to spend it limit their lives, and limit their partner's lives, too, since one of the important functions of money is to enrich and enlarge experience, and make existence more interesting.

A person who gets pleasure from holding on to money may be content simply knowing that it's accumulating in the bank. This kind of activity seldom gets a person into trouble with the real world, although friends may laugh or be envious. However, if the hoarder's desire for money is overwhelming, he or she may do illegal things, like not paying taxes. As all this implies, the partner who isn't tight with money suffers more than the hoarder. Hoarding fulfills some internal need for the hoarder; it brings unnecessary deprivation and perhaps embarrassment to the spouse.

Herman's attitude toward money, for instance, goes back to

the thirties. He thinks money is the central and key ingredient in life. Herman's father "lost everything in the depression." Herman's mother often told him how happy life was when they had money. Herman doesn't remember any of the good times; he only remembers that, when they were poor, life was not happy, and they had no fun, they didn't go anywhere, they didn't do anything, they didn't have friends, they hardly had clothes. Herman's father became a withdrawn, morose, sullen man who sat behind the newspaper and didn't pay any attention to Herman.

Herman's greatest fear is of losing money, and security is his idea of a good life. Herman is a civil servant, and very frugal. An extra serving of French fries at McDonald's requires a family conference about whether it's really worth it. His wife has a job, but he doesn't want her to spend her money any more than he wants to spend the money he earns. Herman is a gentle man, but becomes absolutely enraged at the idea that somebody would want to spend money. Old clothes are fine. Old furniture is better. Food at home is healthier. Why should working people travel? They only get tired. One certainly should be friendly with neighbors, but if you invite them into your house you may have to feed them. Money is to be saved for future security.

The pyschological reasons for these three attitudes toward money—overworking for it, overspending it, and overhoarding—tend to be similar. At a deep unconscious level all three kinds of people believe that money, just money, nothing else but money, will give them their hearts' desire, such as power, or youth, or absolute security, or beauty, or sex appeal. They believe that getting it, having it, spending it will make them more than they are—for instance, more fascinating or more sexually appealing or immune to misfortune.

MONEY AS A WEAPON

Money can also be used as a form of blackmail by one spouse in a marriage to gain domination over the other. In a good marriage, spouses arrive at a mutually acceptable way of handling their assets and will not allow money to become a weapon. In a bad marriage, one partner will use money to control the other, and to keep him or her in a servile position by threatening to withhold it or by promising to give more of it, or sometimes both of these alternatively. It can be used to extract sexual favors from the other partner, even to force the other partner to do abhorrent sexual acts. It can be used as a tool to hold on to the partner's loyalty, or as a bribe to demand the other's time and companionship. All these maneuvers generate tension.

People who use money like this are likely to be those for whom possession of money is the chief or even the only claim to being worthwhile. Some who feel inferior use their money in this distorted way to assume superiority over the spouse; in the process destroying any notion that marriage is a relationship of equals.

Percy, for example, is the breadwinner in his family. He and Evelyn have been married twenty years, and have five children. Evelyn is mother, wife, and homemaker, and Percy is the boss. His earning power, he feels, gives him the right to be boss. He doesn't want to share authority, so he won't even allow Evelyn to earn any money outside the home. He allots the cash, he sets the financial priorities, he says what will be bought when. When Evelyn or the children need anything, they have to go to him and ask for the money to buy it.

Of course, for every partner who uses money to dominate, there has to be a partner who—for lack of money, inability to make it, insecurity, fear, or for a complex of such reasons—allows himself or herself to be abused, perhaps even degraded. This person will inevitably have a bad self-image and ill feelings toward the dominating spouse, including anger, resentment and, sometimes even guilt over being in such an untenable situation. These emotions can lead to severe anxiety and depression, and even other mental illness.

Money is sometimes used to entice a desired person into marriage. The prospect of having money can be very seductive. Marriages honestly contracted on this pragmatic basis can succeed if both partners clearly understand the rules and live by them after the marriage contract is signed. On the other hand, these marriages undertaken for money may involve poorly matched spouses, who differ in their racial, cultural, religious, and educational characteristics, and are therefore more likely to fail. Only if both partners demonstrate decency, loyalty, and a willingness to stick to their monetary bargain, will the bond of affection between them grow.

THE HOME

For many reasons married people have better homes than single people at the same socioeconomic level. It's easy to see why. Married people potentially have two incomes, especially before and after they are raising children. It's even sometimes possible for both to work while the children are growing up. They also are able to tap the resources of one or both sets of their relatives. But what may be more basic is the differences in their priorities. Married people need a home more than single people, so they invest more of their psychological, physical, and financial resources in having one, and keeping it up. Single people typically need to invest their resources in a quest for companionship and sexual fulfillment, and cannot make a home a high-priority item.

Furthermore, a home is central to bringing up children for practical and psychological reasons. Besides providing shelter, it also provides a setting in which parents can demonstrate on a small scale how to handle many of the problems the children will have to face in the world. The way people relate and get along in the family will teach a child how to get along with other people. "In this family we are kind to one another. See how awful it is when your big sister teases you? Now you know what it feels like, so maybe you won't tease your little brother anymore." "If you don't listen to the other person, you won't know what's going on. Now you don't know where your friends have gone to play." "See how messy and uncomfortable the house gets when we all don't cooperate to keep it clean."

"We must all work because otherwise things don't get done soon enough. Mommy has less time to play with you tonight becuase you didn't help her."

A couple's home can become a focus of stress in their marriage when there's either too much or too little involvement in the home. Some people spend much more than they should in order to have a home in a particular neighborhood, furnished in a particular way. It may be a matter of living in the city in spite of inconvenience, crowding, pollution, and high cost, or in a rural setting despite exorbitant commuting time. A couple with young children may insist on furnishing with antiques that they can't afford and that the children are bound to damage. Others are so devoted to tidiness and cleanliness that their house is always on display, the objects are always polished and shined and cannot be used.

Any of these situations may be due simply to poor judgment, a case of not correctly comprehending the reality of the situation. Both spouses have to live with the consequences and, if they agree about what they want, they may get by rather well. Although they will be stressed because of their poor judgment—they will be broke, they will be tired, they won't have time or energy for other things—at least they won't be in conflict over how they want to live.

The situation often becomes dramatically stressful when it is one partner's poor judgment that is at fault—for instance, when a couple invests more in a home than they can afford because one partner insists on it. This may be due to lack of wisdom or simply stupidity, but it often indicates some unconscious need that somehow has not been fulfilled in an appropriate and direct way; the person is trying to fulfill it in an indirect, camouflaged way. A conflict can easily come out in connection with a home because, besides serving the practical needs of shelter, it serves as an arena for the symbolic expression of self—one's interests, tastes, accomplishments, ambitions, desires, needs.

Take the case of the woman who felt unattractive when she was young, because she had never been petted or admired. Her brother was the favorite, and she could not live up to his achievements. When she was an adolescent, she was deeply disappointed by a boy and felt she did not receive the sympathy she should have had. Instead, she felt, she was mocked and ridiculed. As a married women, she filled her house with every possible ornament, ignoring her husband's pleas that they could not afford the expense, and that her expenditures robbed them of vacations and even things their children really needed. She did not know why she did the things she did. She was overcome by an unending desire to have new curtains, new carpets, new wallpaper, new lamps. New possessions only satisfied her for a short time. She tired of her acquisitions quickly and had to replace them with what she called better and more up-to-date things. Her behavior was a way of trying to decorate herself and get compliments on how attractive she was. Somehow her home and its physical appearance symbolically represent her and her appearance.

A man felt dirty because he used to masturbate. He was a nervous little boy and began to play with himself while still very young. His grandmother caught him at it and yelled at him because she said that he was doing something disgusting. She told him that terrible things would happen to him, and frightened him. As a man, he has an impeccable yard. His lawn is a thing of beauty but he never has time to throw a ball to his children or read them a story. He doesn't spend much time with his wife either. They seldom go anywhere at night or even on weekends. He is too tired to make much love but his grass is beautiful, his trees are pruned, his leaves are raked. Also, the house is freshly painted inside and out. He barely finishes painting when he starts again. He is not painting the house. He is ridding himself of his childhood feelings of dirtiness and depravity.

Psychological problems can also show themselves in the opposite way, by neglect, neglect to the point where a request for help around the house is considered a personal assault. Sometimes these people simply refuse to work to help provide a home. In both cases they are in effect refusing to acknowledge the necessity of having a home. Take the woman who knows she has the time and energy to clean her house but doesn't know why she can't bring herself to do it. The rugs are never clean, the bathrooms are filthy, the dishes are in the sink. She remembers that her mother's house was spotless, but also that her mother didn't often kiss her, or hug her, or have time for her; instead, her mother always seemed to be vacuuming the carpets or scrubbing the bathroom. She therefore refuses to clean her house, not because she's too tired or even because she's lazy. Without being aware of it, she is holding out for her mother's love. She hates to clean her house because she sees clean carpets and clean bathrooms as competing for her mother's attention.

A man who has worked hard to provide a nice home for his family now somehow cannot find the time to rake the leaves or clean the gutters or paint the trim. He doesn't know why. He is proud of the fact that he was able to buy a house. He is a good businessman. He does not want his investment to go to waste. But somehow he cannot bring himself to take care of the house, even though his wife asks him to, and he himself feels embarrassed when he looks at how it's deteriorating. He always has something else to do, something else he would rather do. He remembers that, when he was a boy, his father always had time to rake the leaves, but never had time to throw a ball with him; his mother was a busy housekeeper and baked a lot of cookies, but never had time to read to him. He is not aware that now, though he himself is a man, a husband, and a father, he is competing with his house for the love of his parents. Moreover, his parents, it happens, are retired and living in an apartment on the other side of town. There are many things he could do with them now to win their love and esteem, but he's somehow not able to bring himself to do them. He is still primarily concerned with their lack of attention to him in his childhood.

Some people, although they long for a home so they can have a private place of their own, turn it into a public place as soon as they have one. They need a lot of people always milling around—friends, acquaintances, relatives, sometimes even virtual strangers. These people are always visiting, eating at the table, sleeping over. If both partners like to live this way, well and good; but frequently it is just the husband or the wife, not both. The consequent tension destroys the harmony of the marriage, and drains the constant entertainers financially and physically. The one who needs to be surrounded by outside people all the time is often motivated by some unconscious desire for which the entertaining is a substitute that doesn't work—the visitors in fact do not give him or her much pleasure.

In some other marriages, he or she refuses to spend money on the house and tries to block the other partner's doing so, even though they do not lack money. Money may be spent, may even be spent lavishly, but not on the home. The cause of this problem is sometimes that the refusing spouse came from a home where there was little love or happiness and therefore considers a home a worthless investment. Ironically, a person like this is typically blind to the fact that the very refusal to spend on the home contributes to an atmosphere of tension and stress, and thus the home indeed is worthless as an investment.

POSSESSIONS

A home is a major possession requiring a large commitment of time, effort, and money, but other possessions may also cause serious stress in a marriage. Some people, to begin with, are strongly addicted to mechanical gadgets. They buy machine after machine. They replace their appliances frequently. They are fascinated by anything new. They buy much more than they realistically can use or can afford. They are not able to exercise their usual intelligence and judgment about the gadgets because these possessions have a powerful, personal, symbolic value far beyond their real value. For example, gadgets may stand for overcoming a physical handicap. A person who, as a child, was immobilized for a long time with a badly broken bone, osteomyelitis, or some other debilitating illness, such as rheumatic fever, may at that time have become absolutely overwhelmed with the desire for freedom and mobility which are now symbolically expressed as love for gadgets.

Some people often use clothes to overcome doubts and fears about themselves. Clothes are magical possessions for them, capable of compensating them for real or imagined personal failings. Some people actually think their clothes can make them more sexual. People try to prove by their clothes and in the saddest cases, by their clothes alone, that they are artistic, successful, intelligent. Others use jewelry in this way, or books, records, paintings, antiques, stamps, or coins. Other people use activities instead. They become addicted to tennis, or golf, hunting or fishing. There are women who neglect their families in pursuit of antique furniture. There are men who fish or golf almost daily, oblivious to the stress it causes in the rest of their lives. Her neglect and his blindness are signs they may be trying to make up for some real or imagined personal failing or fulfill some deeply rooted covert personal desire. The automobile functions like this, too; it's a lot more than a means of transportation to many people. It stands for success or desirability, for free, undaunted adventure. People come to feel they can obtain such rewards from the ownership of an automobile or, usually, one particular kind of automobile. They will pay more for it than they can afford, spend an inordinate amount of time washing and polishing it, and in general get so involved with it that it becomes a cause of marital discord. That luxury car is a striking example of how the good things in life can stress a marriage.

What do you do when some possession or activity is invested with so much of your husband's or wife's psychic energy that it becomes a problem?

The first thing to do is to realize that the need involved probably goes so deep that it is not amenable to logic, or to asking, begging, demanding, cajoling, nagging, or even threatening. If the need can be understood and accommodated, there may not be anything that you have to do. It's neither possible nor necessary that your spouse has to be totally free of conflicts or neuroses. He or she is entitled to hidden or unfulfilled desires, and most of us carry scars from childhood for which we try to compensate. Besides, possessions and activities are matters of taste, which means they are personal, and not fully rational and realistic. If a spouse's hobby or purchases don't really cause big problems, it is well just to accept them. After all, one of the best ways to show affection and love is to be tolerant, and even peculiar quirks sometimes come to seem charming or even endearing.

If you can't accept, don't berate. If one spouse nags the other about quirks and unconscious needs, the accused spouse is apt to take it as a sign of lack of love and rejection. It is better to learn to live with a mate's behavior than to suffer through marital strife.

Certain irrational needs for possessions or activities may stress a marriage even if they ordinarily are considered to enrich family life—for instance, social service, or collecting beautiful paintings, or buying good books. In these cases, too, it is not the choice that is wrong, but the particular intensity with which it is being pursued. The best approach here is to try to help the spouse who needs the activity become aware that he or she is changing something worthwhile into a problem. This requires uncovering the real source of the intense drive for doing this or having that. Here the services of a psychiatrist can be extremely helpful. Psychiatrists help people understand themselves and their actions. A psychiatrist can help someone see, for instance, that he or she is devoted to helping delinquent youths not because the work is useful and valuable, though it is, but because for some very personal reason, doing so increases a sense of personal power, prestige, and intellectual ability. Such insight makes it possible to see that the level of devotion and quantity of energy expended are actually unrealistic and therefore counterproductive—that is, they work against you, rather than for you.

The activities we have been discussing—work, making and handling money, establishing and keeping up a home, gathering possessions—are aimed at long-term goals. In order to have a chance of being happy, there must be a reasonably close connection between the way these goals can be achieved in the real world and how each of us goes about achieving them. A house by itself cannot generate the atmosphere, the love, the interest, the intellectual excitement we need. It is only a setting. If the effort of paying for the house, or keeping it spotless and repaired, becomes excessive and therefore unrealistic, the house and everything in it will come to be stressful. For a happy life, married couples must pay attention to maintaining a good balance between long-term commitments, everyday pleasures and the gratification of basic, everyday needs.

CHAPTER 6

The Tender Side of Marriage

LOVE AND MARRIAGE

It sounds corny, but it's true—one of the enduring appeals of marriage is love. Marriage encourages the people in it to love each other purely, loyally, and without reservations, and it makes a person feel very special to be able to give and receive that special kind of love.

Today this specialness is a very strong argument for marriage. Much of modern life tends to make people feel less special and important—the number of people in the world, the publicity about others' exploits, the fact that we have begun to explore outer space. This is also true for children. Television shows them other children who appear more interesting than they are themselves. Furthermore, weakened family ties, dispersion of the extended family, upheavals in society, and job mobility contribute to the difficulty of feeling unique, special, or important. Marriage counteracts some of this, because it is easier to maintain self-esteem if it is shared by another.

This sense of being special to someone else is not to be confused with fusion—finding an identity and self-esteem only in and through the other. Married people must have their own individual feelings of identity and self-worth, which can be achieved in many other ways besides being married. Marriage should not be a substitute for other avenues of adult functioning. But a successful loving marriage does help the partners to feel good about themselves, and thus makes it easier for them to be successful in the world.

Marriage is not able to erase ambivalence from love. All love is somewhat ambivalent, and even in the best marriages the spouses doubt, question, and at times, dislike each other.

There are other emotional complications. One partner may have a greater capacity to love than the other, and be markedly more able to show it. The intensity of their love will have highs and lows, changing with their circumstances. These complications may interact with each partner's perception of how much love he or she is receiving or giving, and each one's feelings of satisfaction and disatisfaction about the love in their marriage. This may cause stress.

One sign that a marriage is having trouble is that one partner complains of too little or no love. As I have said, pragmatic loveless marriages can be satisfactory, but most people consider love a necessary ingredient in a marriage. When a partner feels he or she is getting too little or no love, he or she becomes most unhappy. Although they usually say the problem is simply that their spouse does not love them or love them enough, sometimes their own inability to receive love is the source of the difficulty. They may not recognize when love is being shown, for instance, or they may be projecting their own problems with love onto the other person.

The question "Do you love your spouse?" is ordinarily easy to answer. If he or she evokes warm positive feelings plus sexual excitement, generally an essential element of married love, then you do love him or her. The question of whether that love is returned is more complicated. Here you have to understand the way he or she shows love, which is sometimes not easy to do. People who grew up in an atmosphere without much warmth or love, for instance, tend to define love in very rigid and narrow terms, and tend to feel unloved if a spouse doesn't show love in a particular way. Their own ability to give and accept love is also apt to be rather limited, even when they intensely desire to do so.

If people are aware of these psychological factors, they will be less likely to wrongly conclude that their marriage lacks love. We all, in fact, have preconceived and tenacious ideas of what "loving" means. These ideas are for the most part rooted in early childhood, when the way we were treated by the people who took care of us established our adult ability to express affection and the ways we express it. These roots in our early years give these ideas their strong hold on us. Some show love by working hard and bringing home their entire paycheck, others by making a great display of physical affection.

Marcia, for instance, is unhappy because she's sure Seth doesn't love her. Marcia's parents were divorced when she was a little girl. Her mother worked at a job all week, then on Saturday and Sunday she did all the household chores. It seemed to Marcia that her mother's life was very sad. Marcia survived her childhood by daydreaming. She always imagined that, when she grew up, she'd marry a daddy, not a husband, to whom she'd be a mommy, not a wife. What she meant by a daddy was a handsome man like the ones on TV; what she meant by a mommy was a pretty lady with pretty clothes. She thought that she and her daddy would spend a lot of time together, she'd wear beautiful clothes, and they would go out to exciting parties. When her own marriage did not approximate her daydream defined in soap opera terms, Marcia began to feel certain that Seth did not love her.

Roger, too, feels unloved for childhood reasons. His mother worked all day and arranged for him to be taken care of by her neighbor, Mrs. Smith, who had her own little boy Roger's age. Mrs. Smith was not a professional babysitter; she only took care of Roger as a favor to her neighbor. As Roger remembers it, Mrs. Smith was very nice, and seemed absolutely content to be taking care of her house and the two boys. To Roger, being loved by a woman came to mean having Mrs. Smith love you—that is, having a wife who stays home, wears an apron, cooks wonderful food, who kisses you when you come in and pats your head, and whose job it is to take care of you. Roger's wife,

Bridget, however, does none of these things. She's a nurse, and works from seven in the morning to three in the afternoon. She leaves home before six a.m. to be at the hospital at seven. After she finishes her work at the hospital, she does the shopping, which means she usually does not return home much before six. Roger feels terribly unloved and rejected by Bridget. He doesn't care that she contributes money to the family, and that she also manages to keep the house. She doesn't fit his image of Mrs. Smith. She isn't there to greet him when he comes home or to say goodbye when he leaves for work; and she does not spend enough time in the kitchen cooking food. Unfortunately, he doesn't understand why he feels so deeply that Bridget doesn't love him.

To have a good love relationship with any person requires that you accept love in the way he or she shows it. But all is not predetermined; things can be changed. When people feel unloved, it can be very helpful if they talk about it openly and honestly, so that the spouse can learn how to demonstrate love in ways that will be meaningful.

Often one partner's complaint of too little love goes hand in hand with the other's complaint that too much love is being demanded. Essentially this is a complaint that one spouse is making restrictive and confining demands on the other. There is a difference between loving a person and being highly possessive and demanding. It is not love to use anyone else to fulfill all your emotional needs. It is not love to demand constant nurturing. All adults must assume responsibility for their own functioning. Also, all adults need to be loved in a way that does not interfere with their capacities. On the other hand, the complaint may also mean that a spouse's appropriate wishes for affection, time, reassurance, support, and attention are interpreted as an attack on the other's options. People have to be careful that when they complain of excessive and restrictive demands for love, they are not blaming someone else for their own limitations that they are unable to face.

In fact, stress over love in a marriage is usually a two-way street. Both partners have trouble accepting each other's needs, and therefore have trouble being supportive and reassuring. To avoid such a situation, remember how necessary it is to accept differences, and don't be embarrassed to show love and support. It takes time to work out a love relationship. It helps to be open and honest, to be willing to expose yourselves to one another, or to be frank about each other. As your dialogue goes on, be patient and as generous as possible with time and affection. It is important to learn to listen, not just lecture. What the other person is saying may be valid. Realize that you are not always the best perceiver of yourself or your mate. Of course, open communication does not signify that you agree with all you're hearing. It does mean that you are willing to listen and learn.

Peter, for example, will not listen to his wife. Maude is a quiet, tense, shy woman; she can show strength and determination, but doing so drains her emotional resources. Peter's business took him to the city where Maude was a school teacher, and they knew one another for years before they married. On each date with Peter, Maude looked elegant. Peter was impressed by her but he had no idea how long it took her to get ready to see him. Maude wanted to marry Peter who, after much hesitation, finally agreed. Ever since, Peter sees her as a very strongly determined woman who wants her own way and gets it. Peter saw his mother dominate his father, and he is determined that no woman will do the same to him. He views any show of emotion in a man as a weakness and as an opening that allows a woman to get the upper hand. He really does not understand that Maude is shy and that she worries a great deal and needs his support. He refuses to believe that she's so tense, because it frightens him. He deals with it by turning away, ignoring it, and burying himself in his work. Maude, in turn, feels rejected, unloved, and therefore depressed. She has tried to talk to Peter, but all attempts on her part to communicate with him about emotional issues, about love and affection, threaten him, so that he withdraws. If she persists, he grows angry and says she's nagging.

Hazel has another kind of problem with communicating. She grew up thinking that when people care for one another they are always aware of each other's wishes. As a married woman, she's finding that it doesn't necessarily work that way. Her husband is forceful and dominant; she relies heavily on him and, when they married, she simply assumed that, since he was wiser and better educated, he would understand her completely. She has a lot of trouble telling him how she feels and what she wants because of her assumption that if he truly loved her, he would automatically understand what she wants and needs and give it to her. She finds it particularly difficult to express herself if her feelings are negative; nonetheless, she gets hurt, resentful, and angry if her unspoken hostility is not taken into account.

COMPANIONSHIP IN MARRIAGE

The companionship offered by a good, compatible, sexually active marriage is multidimensional, encompassing all areas of life, and having the special glow of sexual attraction. A good friend does not have to be of the opposite sex, but the companionship of one who is, is especially rewarding. To be deprived of companionship in marriage leads to feelings of loneliness and rejection.

The quantity of time spent together and the kinds of activities shared will differ with each couple. Some have similar interests and desires, and spend much time together. Others are highly invested in individual activities, and the partners do not have to share large amounts of time. Some married people merely have to know that their spouse loves them and will be available when needed. All that matters is that the arrangement is satisfactory to both partners.

In a culture like ours that places such importance on individuality, couples who spend a great deal of time together are often regarded with amazement, envy, or, sometimes, contempt. If their life is harmonious this way, however, their closeness is right and healthy for them. But they will be less able to grow individually and independently, and they do face the risk that when one of them dies, the partner may be less able to cope with living alone since he or she will have had relatively little experience of it, and will have developed relatively few skills for doing it.

Couples like this are out of step with our society, which encourages autonomy, independence, and the development of individual skills in as many areas as possible. Couples who spend most of their time together, including those who work with each other and share almost all activities, are thus in a minority. But that doesn't matter, as long as they are doing what is right for them. They find it much more fun to do things together, and they do not feel lonely or neglected, or taken advantage of because their spouses get to do more interesting things.

Even if a couple is almost constantly together, it will not put stress on their marriage as long as they both find this state of affairs satisfactory.

Companionship may involve stress, however, if the desire for it is unequal—that is, if one spouse desires it much more than the other. If one partner has strong personal needs to pursue certain interests independently, whether these be professional, financial, recreational, political, or social, and the other partner is not able to understand and support these activities, the uninvolved spouse will feel neglected, in competition with the activities and jealous of them. This situation is one of the most common causes of marital discord. Usually, neither spouse wants to end the marriage; rather, both are interested in going on together. Neither has done anything that the other finds unforgivable or irreparable; still, they find themselves locked into a very painful situation that causes them to have harsh feelings toward one another. They are not able to understand how they got there, but their affection for each other is eroding.

Of course it is natural and right to expect that marriage will at least partly fulfill needs for companionship. When these needs are unmet, there is reason to feel frustrated and stressed. But the first question to be asked is, why does one partner not spend time with the other, or not enough time to gratify the other?

If one partner has intense separate interests and needs to spend only limited time with the other partner, the couple may be mismatched in energy level, interest level, or intelligence.

Or, one or the other may have psychological problems. If there is affection and concern in the marriage, the one who is greatly engrossed in some activity outside the marriage will know that it is causing pain and deprivation to someone he or she loves, yet still be unable to curtail the activity. It is clear that he or she is investing a lot of psychological energy in this activity, and indeed may be trapped into doing it by internal problems and be unable to work free. In the last chapter, I pointed out that this kind of involvement in activity is often fueled by an unconscious, misconceived effort to solve some personal problem. The psychological mechanism at work here can be very powerful. Some people suffer if they cannot follow these interests; their activities maintain their very identity. They will feel attacked and will respond with rage if they are forbidden to continue to devote their time and energy to them.

A different reason for this kind of marital problem is that one partner has personally underinvested in the world at large, has not developed his or her personal interests, and so is too dependent for reassurance and fulfillment on the presence of the other partner. In short, one clings to the other.

Often people find themselves in this situation for reasons that have nothing to do with normal companionship. Clinging people often have great fears of something in life that they are trying, sometimes desperately, to avoid facing alone. They are not likely to admit to this. They don't say, "Please stay with me, I've got this terrible anxiety"; instead, they camouflage their need with apparently reasonable requests for companionship, or, sometimes, personal criticism. "It's really unkind of you to go to all of those awful ball games."

Clinging can be a very destructive form of relating. It is parasitic. It drains and constricts the other partner. The marriage begins to look like a prison; the clinging partner is a guard always watching the other, the prisoner, for fear he or she will escape from this enforced togetherness.

Of course the other partner wants to escape, but how? The person who seeks the togetherness can't say why. Unless the other is very perceptive and unusually kind, he or she is likely to see the clinging person's behavior as mean or vindictive, and react accordingly. "She browbeats me to stay home." Such a marriage often develops into a sick, twisted relationship in which neither person is free to develop fully as a complete, independent, interesting adult. In some relationships, neither partner can stand aloneness, but in different contexts—he wants to be constantly with her at home, say, and she is afraid to go downtown by herself—and so each demands too much companionship at different times. This is very far from the secure but liberating companionship that marriage is capable of providing!

Married people are often amazed that they can be so unhappy when their problem is merely disharmony in their needs for companionship. Yet this disharmony often does play havoc with the quality of their lives. A companionship problem is sinister and insidious; people have time to see it growing and to think about it, and when they become aware that they seem to be heading for a disaster, they often consult a psychiatrist.

In treating these couples, it is necessary first to understand how far outside the usual norms they are. How much is the more independent partner, man or woman, involved in activities outside the marriage? If it is a great amount, are the activities invested with unrealistic psychological content that may make them intractable, so that there are apt to be continuing problems in the marriage? Is the unfulfilled partner clinging and dependent? If so, how much so? Are the unfulfilled partner's needs actually within the usual bounds or are they excessive? Do they amount to neurotic needs—that is, is this someone who is trying to use the spouse as an ego booster, as a shield against the world, as a means of overcoming all fears and frustrations?

Of course, these are all value judgments, since there are no absolutes, no definite guidelines, no specific formulas. The problem revolves around what is not enough or too much companionship; what is just the right amount is merely what is comfortable in the particular marriage. What the partners must strive for is a working arrangement in which both feel free to pursue individual interests so that their identities are not threatened, and yet there is enough time to spend together so that each partner's companionship needs are met. In marital therapy, it isn't only a question of how optimally healthy or realistic the partners can become, but rather how they can be helped to become better suited to one another. In essence, how can they be helped not to be threatened by one another's internal needs, neurotic or not, and so become able to be more supportive of each other?

RECREATION IN MARRIAGE

Though both partners in a marriage should pursue their own interests and not view each other's interests as rivals, a marriage in which the interests are so different and the tastes so opposite that the couple cannot play together will have problems. It is part of a good relationship to be able to spend at least some leisure time playfully together, relaxing in one another's company, taking part in enjoyable activities together, and adding to each other's enjoyment of them. When the partners always or even mostly go their own recreational ways, the marriage is impoverished. Recreation may not be at the core of a good marriage, but it is certainly a very nice bonus.

It is not always only different interests that cause problems here. Recreation, to be recreation, must involve a change, a break in routine. Someone who sits at a desk all day may find it very refreshing to jog around the block. Someone who spends the day carrying heavy loads at a construction site is likely to prefer to sit quietly watching TV. Most wives and husbands spend much of their time so differently that they may not always be able to find a situation that is a change of pace for both of them. Women who spend their days at home want to get out of the house. Men who spend their time elsewhere during working hours want to relax at home. Men who eat in restaurants during their work day are likely to look forward to an evening meal at home. Women who eat at home all the time look forward to a chance to go out to a restaurant.

Recreation can become a serious stress on a marriage when it is used to compensate for something else, or when too much time, effort, and energy are devoted to it. The two problems often go together. Recreation helps soothe us from the disappointments, insults, and other psychological bruises of daily life; but that's all recreation can do, it cannot heal those bruises. An executive becomes president of his club rather than president of his company, which is what he really wants to be. His recreation is a useful outlet for his frustration. But when recreation is used to fulfill needs because the normal channel through which they would be fulfilled is blocked, judgement of reality often suffers and people are likely to spend great amounts of time and energy pursuing rootless fantasies and desires through recreation.

Take Nat. He's a technician in a large chemical company. He does not have a college degree. He feels blocked, frustrated, and ignored. His work is only a job. He lives for his weekends which he spends fishing and hunting. He belongs to a sports club where he feels like a man, an appreciated peer. His time at the club plays a major part in his life. His wife is extremely proud of him, and she doesn't understand why he's so unhappy at work, since she thinks he has a good job. Nat's problem is that he didn't like school and wasn't a good student, especially not in math. Now he's in the situation where the same boys who were good in school have all the best jobs, and he's working for them. He sees fishing and hunting as the only opportunities he has to be a man among peers. His wife sees these activities as rivals. She resents the money he spends on them, and resents the time that he spends away from her.

Some individuals feel that if they could spend all their time in recreation, they would be totally happy. Of course recreation cannot make people happy. All it can do is make them feel more relaxed, refreshed, amused, or diverted. To be happy we have to perform well in various areas of life, not simply in one only and particularly not in one so full of fantasy and fleeting joy as recreation. Many people have trouble comprehending this. They feel that recreational activities are supposed to and will make them happy, and that the more of these activities they have, the happier they will be.

Of course there are married people among them, and sometimes both spouses, not just one, try to use recreation to achieve this illusory goal. In general, if both have the same poor judgment and they like to indulge in recreation together, their marriage will be stressed by the consequences of this mutual poor judgment, and not by disagreement. If they go separate ways or if only one of them is overinvolved in recreation, they are likely to disagree. Whether they fight or get along, their marriage will be seriously stressed because they will spend an excessive amount of time, energy, and probably money on recreational activity. Married people who live for recreation neglect other family members, as well as marital and other interests and duties. On top of this, as with anyone who lives this way, they drain their physical and emotional strength. All their playing leaves them, not feeling refreshed and relaxed and able to go full steam ahead to take care of other activities, as people should feel after recreation, but drained and exhausted.

The kind of people who use recreation for unhealthy internal reasons tend to have a low frustration tolerance—that is, they find the pursuit of long-term goals difficult and painful. To get around this difficulty they seek fulfillment through recreation and come to view it as the main purpose of living. This leads to neglecting such things as working, paying the family bills, taking care of the home, and spending time with whomever they are married to.

People with low frustration tolerance also may hurt their marriages because their idea of recreational activity is apt to involve seeking thrills. Wild thrill seeking in sensational activities is often very detrimental to a marriage for the simple reason that it brings a large element of risk into it. Thrill seekers delight in gambling, where the thrill comes from the financial risks they take, sometimes tremendous risks. Gambling obviously can have serious repercussions for a marriage. Or the thrills may be dangerous to their health and very lives, which puts a serious burden of continuing anxiety on their spouses and children.

Sometimes two thrill seekers get married. They may both sense that neither of them can cope with the serious demands of adulthood, come to a harmonious agreement that the wild activities they crave are indeed worthwhile, and then live by that agreement. Although they are not likely to succeed in terms of longterm goals, at least they don't fight with one another over the risks they bring into their life together, but rather support one another in taking chances.

SUPPORT IN ADVERSITY

Other people besides a spouse can be of help during times of adversity, but their aid is never quite the same. The institution of marriage is uniquely geared to be supportive in times of disaster. The marriage is made for better or worse, through sickness and health, for richer, for poorer. In a good marriage this commitment is fortified by mutual love and esteem. Even a marriage that is not very good is fortified by what the spouses have in common simply through being married—the same children, jointly owned property, insurance policies, work commitments, in short, the partnership arrangements of a married life. And life being what it is, it can be expected that each spouse will have a chance to repay the other for kindness shown during a period of personal crisis.

Behind the partnership arrangements of marriage stand the social customs and laws that support them. They serve to discourage any tendency of a fragile spouse to be disloyal or abandon a mate in difficult times. Under pressure many people behave weakly; they succumb to their ambivalence and their own fears. Social pressure as well as the marital arrangement itself help even some quite frail people become strong and firm, supportive and sustaining.

At the heart of the capacity to support a spouse is the positive relationship that exists on so many levels when people are happily wed. Even in fortunate times people function better when they have love, security, companionship, and a sexual outlet. When misfortune strikes, you need even more the love, security, companionship, and sex a good marriage gives. When you are going through a crisis and you are distraught, drained, and afraid, your spouse will be lover, companion, and loyal friend.

These advantages persist no matter how long the marriage lasts or how old the partners become. People who move smoothly and healthily from one age to the next are those who lay down a foundation in one period of life to prepare themselves for the next. The reason long-term goals are so important is that they help us do this, by allowing us some sense of stability from one age to another, and this helps cushion our perceptions of change.

Various other things help, too. People who take good care of themselves—who eat properly, rest enough, exercise, and do not abuse their bodies with drugs or alcohol—tend to take healthy bodies from age to age. People who have developed social or work skills of lasting value are able to age more gracefully. People who have healthy relationships find that these help. And so do good marriages. Successfully married people grow older with the following advantages: They have a much better than average chance of not being lonely. They have the emotional security that comes from having somebody to love and be loved by, plus the security of having a partner with whom to share the tasks of adulthood. They have someone to take over should they meet disaster—illness, either their own or that of some other important member of the family, great financial adversity, and so forth. They have somebody to have sex with and can be pretty confident they will be able to stay sexually active indefinitely as they grow older.

Short-term relationships can be exciting, intense, and tender. There is a great joy just in getting to know another person intimately and experiencing the unexpected. But there are precious qualities that can only be part of a close relationship that has lasted a long time, a combination of intensity, deep knowledge, and comfort that comes from having spent a great deal of time together and having worked through together the countless problems of daily life as well as more extraordinary problems. As people grow older, they inevitably become less resilient and more fixed in their ways. It is harder to venture out and meet new people and start new relationships. It's a joy to have a partner who knows you very well and accepts you as you are, and about whom you feel the same. It's a tremendous advantage to have spent years with someone while both of you have changed and matured.

The average life span of the American male is seventy-two years, of the American woman, seventy-six years. After they are forty years old, average Americans live more than thirty years. This means that for the major part of life, when you no longer possess the stamina, vigor, curiosity, and adventurousness of youth, it becomes increasingly sadder and more difficult to stand alone in the world. If you are fortunate enough to have a happy, good marriage, middle and old age can be rich and full.

CHAPTER 7

Partners In Marriage

AM I RIGHT FOR MARRIAGE?

Besides considering the advantages of marriage, and the functions it performs, people thinking of marriage must also evaluate themselves as honestly as they can. Certain personality characteristics help to make people suitable for marriage; those who have them are better candidates for it than those who don't.

Capacity for Intimacy. One of the most important qualities to a person entering marriage is a capacity for intimate relationships. Marriage promises an intimate relationship, but people vary in their capacity to handle intimacy. It is therefore important to know your own capacity for intimacy, and whether you view such a relationship as a prison, or as a liberating force.

Many people are frightened by intimacy and security; they equate love and caring with danger. They have problems with dependency and independency needs. We all have a need to be dependent, to be loved, taken care of, made to feel secure. But also we all have a need to be independent, to be daring, brave, adventurous, or even just private. There is no ideal balance between these contrary needs, or even any way to quantify the balance. It varies from person to person and varies in the same person at different ages. Contrast, for example, the reasons for Chester's and Rick's attitudes.

Chester is a highly educated, successful, cultured man with impeccable manners. He has had friends for many years, but these relationships are not really intimate. His friends are also successful men who live all over the country, and who meet only occasionally, for a good time. Chester has a cordial relationship with his father, but they are not really very close. He loves his mother and admires her, but because she has domineering ways, he considers her dangerous. She nags and wants to know everything he does. He has always maintained a good relationship with her only by keeping her uninformed. He loves his wife, but she wants him to be more open with her, and share with her his feelings, thoughts, ideas, hopes. He finds her wish for intimacy enormously threatening, suffocating, and imprisoning. He is, as it happens, loyal to her, and actually has no major secrets from her; yet he rejects her need for closeness and intimacy as an invasion of his privacy.

Rick, on the other hand, is a very dependent person who is trying to appear independent, rather than, like Chester, being afraid of losing his individual identity. Rick is a successful businessman, active, vigorous, involved in many ventures. He spoils his wife, giving her expensive gifts and indulging her in everything she wants to do. Actually, Rick's indulgence and his encouragement of a very active social life, are both designed to keep his wife happy and busy, so that he's always sure of her. With Rick's dependency needs taken care of, he is able to use his work to express his needs for independence.

Marie's life shows what happens when one partner makes excessive and inappropriate demands on the other because of dependency needs. Marie has many fears. She can't ride in an elevator, on a train, or in an airplane. She is able to camouflage these fears because these devices do not play a major role in her life. She is, however, also uncomfortable in cars and therefore has not been able to learn to drive, which is enormously inconvenient since she lives in the suburbs. Marie tries to hide her fears and pretend there is nothing wrong with her. She reacts to any mention of them with rage. She uses her phobias as a way to justify and excuse her total dependence on her husband. He has to take her everywhere and must be with her almost all the time. If he has anything else he must do, she screams at him for being thoughtless and selfish. These are not legitimate requests for support and acceptance, but expressions of problems she is unable to handle.

What is necessary is to be aware that both needs exist; that the equilibrium between them will inevitably change; and that we are always going to feel some conflict between them. People who are well suited for marriage have a healthy recognition of both these needs and do not claim to be more dependent or independent than they are. Nobody is either totally dependent or totally independent, and marriage suits those who want to have both needs fulfilled through an intimate relationship with another person.

There are people who believe that any love relationship is dangerous. They believe that, if you love someone, your happiness depends on them and then, if you lose them, you will be unhappy. They are usually not good candidates for marriage. Although they pretend to be very independent, in reality they have huge dependency needs. They are so terrified of being abandoned that they cannot become close to anyone. And so they bring on themselves the very condition of which they are most terrified, that of being alone.

Connie, for instance, is someone who is afraid of love because it makes a person vulnerable. Connie is a very pretty girl, and likes men very much. But as soon as a boyfriend begins to tell her how special she is, how wonderful she is, what she means to him, and particularly when he tries to find out if she sees anyone else, she becomes uncomfortable and drops him. Sometimes she misses him and has a hard time until she forgets him, but still she will drop him. Connie's father was killed when she was eight years old; the family moved in with her mother's parents and then, when Connie was thirteen, her grandfather died. After that, life became very difficult. As far as Connie is concerned, love is dangerous, because it makes you dependent on men, who then seem to get sick and die.

Other poor marital candidates are those who have strong needs for independence in the sense of needing to pursue very individualistic interests. In marriage, such a person seeks not a partner, but a readily available person who will be subservient and helpful, while he or she is free to push onward in some fascinating activity.

If, then, you are capable of intimacy and look forward with pleasure and only a slight tinge of fear to sharing time, activities, and aspirations with one special, beloved person, marriage will be the right life style for you. As part of intimacy, of course, you also have to accept the mutuality of needs, that is, be willing to take into account your partner's wishes and needs. Without the willingness to accept that mutuality and accommodate to it, a marriage will not work.

Tolerance for Frustration. Tolerance for frustration is also important. People with low frustration tolerance by and large do not make good marital partners. A long-term commitment with long-term goals does not give gratification at all times and under all circumstances. Someone who thinks in long-range terms is not addicted to immediate gratification, and has a high frustration tolerance. What is needed is a good balance between these aspects of personality. It is best if you are neither a person who cannot play and who postpones pleasure indefinitely, nor one who is always playing and who wants immediate gratification and pleasure.

Dick's marriage illustrates what it means to have a low tolerance for frustration. He is always looking for something new, something exciting. He cannot find it in his job except for the rare times he is promoted, so he turns to other things. He buys new clothes; he starts new hobbies, he likes to gamble. He is bored easily, and he constantly seeks new adventures. His wife loves him very much, but has learned the hard way that he never sticks to anything he begins, that he has great difficulty putting into action any plans they make. He loves to dream, but he does not have the patience to do what is necessary to make his dreams a reality.

Oversensitivity. Secure people are much better marital candidates than insecure people. They have a clear picture of themselves and their priorities and interests, they are not easily frightened, and they do not feel easily taken advantage of.

Insecure people tend to describe themselves as very sensitive, but usually this is a most peculiar sensitivity. It is lopsided—a sensitivity to themselves, their needs, their desires, coupled with gross insensitivity to other people's needs. Oversensitive people are forever ready to test the other person in an intimate relationship. They think they are testing the other person's decency, dedication, and love; what they are actually doing is setting a trap for the other person. Sometimes the tester will say, "Why do you interrupt me? You don't find me interesting, you don't listen to me"; the next time, "Why don't you say something? Doesn't what I have to say deserve a comment?" All areas of the relationship are appropriate and fair testing grounds, from the most serious to the most intimate to the most trivial, because the tester sees himself or herself as put upon and vulnerable everywhere. It is impossible for the other person to live up to their expectations, because the oversensitive partner continues to devise new tests of devotion, without ever informing the other person that he or she is being tested, let alone how. Sooner or later the other person fails, either on a technicality, as it were, or by becoming fed up.

It is extremely useful to know whether you are oversensitive like this. A natural way to find out is to review your past relationships and see whether a large number of them ended in failure. If so, what could have been the cause of the failure? Does the answer repeatedly tend to be that the other person was insensitive, or proved to be untrustworthy, unreliable, uncouth, or unloving? If it seems that many relationships have come to a sad end for these reasons, there is a good chance that the problem does not lie in the other person, but that you are setting impossible goals for the other person and so run a high risk of being a very difficult marital partner. If you decide you are responsible, that you do behave like this, psychiatric treatment may be of help. At any rate, it's better to learn about it before marriage than after.

Ken is a person who has a problem getting along with other people. He hopes to be married, and knows exactly what kind of wife he is ready for and what kind of marriage they are going to have. So far, however, Ken doesn't even have a girlfriend, and indeed has very few friends.

Ken is excessively reliable and responsible, and is proud of it. He always awakes at the same time, and catches the same train. He is never late for work. He always has a cup of coffee and reads the paper before work. He always catches the same train home. He is never late for dinner. He doesn't go out much at night; he spends the evenings preparing for the next day, does his paper work, pays his bills, and writes the necessary birthday and anniversary cards for his family. He is lonely, but he consoles himself self-righteously with the knowledge that he doesn't waste time, that he maintains his priorities, and that he has his life under control.

Why isn't this paragon of virtue appreciated by people? Why does he have so few friends? He wonders that himself and explains it by saying that most people do not understand his worth and appreciate his values. Ken does not see that he is rigid, that his life is sterile, that he has left no room in his life for adventure or even spontaneity. He thinks everyone should like what he likes; he has one standard of behavior, his own. He considers himself sensitive to what is right, and everybody else insensitive. Some psychiatric treatment may be of help. At any rate, if you can learn about your own oversensitivity before marriage much grief can be spared.

Egocentricity. Another quality that is not favorable for marriage is extreme egocentricity. Frequently this is the result of unfortunate childhood experiences, either excessive indulgence or excessive harshness. Regardless of reason, people who consider themselves the center of the universe, which in essence means people who see the world as being there for the fulfillment of their own needs, make poor marital partners. Marriage is not the right life style for people who, regardless of what work or play they are involved in, are concerned primarily with what it can do for them and do not get pleasure or fulfillment from mutuality, giving, sharing. People who are aware that this tends to be true for them ought to question whether they should marry. If they are capable of realizing and accepting their egocentricity, they can and should also realize that they are likely to be very difficult mates.

Owen, for example, is extremely egocentric and selfish. He was his parents' first child, and always got his way with his parents, who thought he was wonderful. Owen is intelligent and capable. He has a good job, and spends everything he makes on himself and his own pleasure. He would like to have a wife, because she would be a desirable possession and would devote herself exclusively to fulfilling his every wish and making sure that he is happy. Owen thinks that he is ready for marriage, but he clearly does not understand what marriage is all about.

Physical Aspects. People who take care of themselves physically usually make better marital partners. Naturally we all age over the years, but it is useful to try to keep your body in as good shape as possible. A very important aspect of marriage is sexuality and sensuality, and it is only decent and sensible to try to keep yourself desirable, nice to touch, to hold, to kiss, to hug.

On the other hand, narcissistic self-adoration to the exclusion of other people or other interests is detrimental to marriage, as well as a futile endeavor. There is no way to stop the physical changes that happen to us all. We may be able to slow them down, but we cannot prevent them, and to be preoccupied with trying is foolish. Furthermore, since married life means mutuality and sharing, it is also necessary to accept the same changes in the other person.

Maturity. A very serious pitfall is the fantasy that marriage will be ideal. We have all at times reacted to life's disappointments and problems by daydreaming about a future when all our problems will magically disappear and we'll find ourselves someplace where everything will be just what we want it to be. Many people assume marriage will be this utopia, where they will live in total happiness with the ideal partner. The two of them will love each other purely; no harsh words will ever be exchanged. One look and each will know exactly what the other desires and immediately share the same wish. Together they will overcome all obstacles. At the same time, of course, this marriage will be affluent; they will live in a magnificent home to which they drive in fabulous cars, and where their life will be devoted only to pleasure. This fantasy, of course, provides much room for disappointment, which is later blamed on the marriage.

Marriage is no utopia but a contractual arrangement undertaken by people on this earth. No marriage can fulfill all of our fantasies. Furthermore, idealizing marriage does not equip people to deal with and get the most out of it. Instead, it defeats them, makes it harder for them to use judgment, flexibility, and good sense. Their powers of observation are diminished because they are no longer open-minded, but full of preconceived ideas of how things are going to be; consequently, they find it harder to realize what is actually happening.

Individual differences in self-awareness are enormous. Some people achieve it at an early age; some people never know themselves. Sometimes people can only become aware of themselves with professional help. You need an open mind more than anything else, and even though the process of self-evaluation is never perfect, you should keep on trying. It is never too late to start introspection and self-examination. The earlier you become knowledgeable about yourself, the greater your chances of avoiding mistakes; self-knowledge is a great asset at any age.

Having said all this, I must also warn you not to approach marriage with fussy, over-meticulous planning. No matter how hard we try, we can never make every external circumstance perfect, or entirely right. The human quality of ambivalence is forever present inside us.

I'm certainly not saying that you can foretell the future or visualize exactly how you will react to your marriage. I am only suggesting that before you are married, you should attempt to explore and learn to know yourself, because this cannot help but have much practical value. If you don't understand yourself and what you're seeking in marriage, it will be much harder for you to ensure a good marriage by choosing an appropriate partner.

WHO WOULD BE RIGHT FOR ME?

Unconscious Elements in Selecting a Spouse. The selection of a spouse, one of the most crucial choices of adult life, is an extremely complicated matter. The factors that go into it are many, and many of them are beyond our control. Prominent among these factors are the unconscious elements of the human mind, which partly mold most of our choices. We are never fully aware of why we make a particular choice. Certain feelings and thoughts locked deep in our unconscious mind contribute to our choices, making the world look the way it does to us. Some of our feelings are not realistic or appropriate, and yet they are enduring and compelling; furthermore, since we are not consciously aware of them, they are not amenable to reason. When large areas of mental processes are conflicted and therefore repressed, hidden in the unconscious, people are often quite unaware why what appeals to them does so—they don't know why it turns them on, and drives them. People with more of their mentation available to their conscious awareness and therefore open for their inspection and evaluation, generally are considered to have good judgment and a clear picture of what is real. But nobody is without unconscious thoughts and motivations, and everybody's choices are to some degree influenced by them. Psychiatric treatment can make more of what is unconscious conscious, but under no circumstances do we ever reach that level of grace where all that is unconscious becomes conscious.

The influence of unconscious motivation in the selection of a marital partner is enormous. Some of the most important factors that go into choosing a partner—factors that influence with whom you will fall in love and what will make you feel sexually excited—are too deep for us to ever identify. Many of our sensual tastes spring from our very early sensual experiences as babies and are locked in our unconscious. The experience that is called "love at first sight" is a response to the sensual qualities of another that have the capacity to stimulate a person; exactly which qualities these are was determined in the earliest babyhood of that person, or in his or her childhood.

The unconscious holds memories of dominant past experiences and their consequences. Certain fragments of these memories slip into consciousness and are applied in a noncritical way to current events and experiences. Often, the application to the current situation is not only out of context but also inappropriate. For example, let us say a boy's infancy and early childhood are marred by fighting between his parents. His mother is despondent, often crying, preoccupied with her own thoughts, and unable to respond to him warmly and attentively. It happens that she has brown hair. As an adult man he is excited and stimulated only by blondes, firmly believing that blondes are livelier, more giving, and warmer than women with brown hair. Or, to take another example, say a little girl's father is preoccupied with his work and away from home a lot. When he is at home he's too tired to play with her. He is of medium height and rather heavy. This little girl as a woman firmly believes that tall, slender men are the only ones who are warm, giving, and therefore good lovers. Of course people who for unconscious reasons attribute certain desirable or undesirable mental or emotional qualities to certain physical types, as in these two examples, hamper their quest for and ability to select an appropriate husband or wife.

Matilda, for instance, had a poor childhood. Her father died when she was young, and her mother had to struggle to feed and clothe the children. Matilda's memories of her dad are that he was a gentle man, patient and kind to her; her mother, on the other hand, was harried, impatient, and always too busy. Matilda promised herself that when she grew up she would not be poor, and that she would marry a man who was able to make a good living and who also would have all her father's gentle qualities. She married a successful businessman but now hates it when her husband has to travel on business, hates the hustle and bustle of his life, and hates the fact that he wants her to keep up with him. That reminds her of her mother, and makes her like him less.

The fact that the unconscious affects the way we make choices does not mean that conscious, logical thinking plays no part at all in the process. Indeed, it is necessary to make the conscious mind function to its fullest extent, because the more you're aware that certain things in the unconscious have a powerful influence, the more you can guard against them. Wishes and passions will continue to sit in the unconscious and exert a powerful influence; but you can learn to live with this fact and at times even accommodate it.

In the selection of a marital partner, these unconscious determinations are doubly important because they apply to both people. Remember, any person you are thinking of marrying also has an unconscious that you must try to take into account and understand.

Conscious Elements in Selecting a Spouse. The conscious elements of any partner's personality will be easier to deal with, since they're open to bargaining and accommodation, change and compromise, but you must at the same time pay attention to whatever signs you can see of his or her unconscious wishes, passions, and temptations. These are extremely difficult to change, and if you cannot accommodate to them before marriage, later on they will be a great burden. That is why a period of courtship is necessary—that is, a period of time when you can get to know one another. A marriage is not apt to succeed if the people marry for the wrong reasons or with the wrong set of expectations; therefore, the prospective mates need time to get to know one another, to evaluate one another, to compare themselves with one another and with other people they know, in order to decide if they have enough in common for a marriage. Such deliberation before marriage may seem an old-fashioned idea; however, the more aware you are of what you're doing when you make the choice of a marital partner, the greater the chance you have of its being a good choice, and the better able you will be to handle its consequences.

We all know people who claim that they would very much like to be married, and who are simply waiting for the "right person" who somehow never comes along. This is not a particularly healthy approach to mating. It is healthy to be able to make choices knowing full well that there could be other choices; it's not healthy to be immobilized by the fear that this particular choice is somehow not right, that it may not be the perfect choice, that something better is waiting around the corner. Life moves on and people who wait for the magical moment may never see it.

Just as it's healthy to be able to find a job and devote yourself to it, even though you know full well that it may not be the only or the most perfect job, so, too, in searching for a mate, it's healthy to truly believe that the purpose of the search is to find someone. The success of the search and fulfillment in marriage do not exclusively depend on finding the *only* right person. They also depend on the fact that the person who's searching has a realistic picture of the world, a clear perception of what he or she is looking for, and of what is possible.

In part, the selection of a spouse is a biological phenomenon, just as it is for other living creatures. One person in the biological pool of the species finds another, a stranger of the opposite sex, through some kind of mutual attraction—something that intrigues, excites, stimulates both of them. The attraction should have large aspects of sensuality and sexuality, for only when they are present will the pair have a good and fulfilling sex life. If you choose a spouse without desiring him or her, you are condemning yourself to a sex life that—regardless of training by sex clinics, or sex literature, or pornography, or other paraphernalia—will lack spontaneity and magic. Since a good sex life is extremely enriching and fulfilling, and makes your life much happier, that's a high price to pay for such a choice.

We do not live by sex and sensuality alone and, since marriage is to last for many years, other human needs must also be taken into account so that they too can be fulfilled. This is where the process of selection necessarily becomes more complex. The couple has to exchange ideas and observe each other in various situations in order to arrive at some joint understanding and evaluation of how they would cope with the other aspects of living. How do they express love? What does it mean to each one? What gestures by the other do they each experience as loving and tender? What makes each of them feel secure? How do they express this need, and what will each require from the other to feel secure?

Even sexuality and sensuality need such conscious attention. What does each desire in sex? What does each want to give and to receive, what can each give and not give, what does each refuse to give? How important is sensuality—sights, sounds, smells, tastes, touch—to each of them?

Some understanding of whether they will be able to fulfill each other's needs for companionship is also necessary. Again, what is each willing and able to give? How do they fit into each other's patterns of life? What are his and her needs for recreation, work, achievements and rewards? What does each expect and hope to achieve financially? What kinds of possessions does each want to have in their home? What are each one's aspirations about children and parenthood? Are they both willing to think about and make some provisions for illness, adversity of other kinds, the relentless biological progressions from one time of life to the next?

Nor should they ignore their present physical attributes—health, strength, age—or indeed any other attributes. Each must look at the total person—race, religion, political views, intellectual abilities, education, work capabilities or limitations, interests, talents or lack of talents—because everything that is important about each of them will have repercussions on the other throughout marriage. For the marriage to last and be successful, the partners must be prepared to handle these repercussions at least fairly well.

For several reasons, many people are afraid to get to know their potential mate this way during courtship. They don't want to question the value of the other person as a love object, negating their own passion or the fact that they fell in love with the other person. The don't want to be accused of prying or spying. In fact, seeking the truth and trying to adust to it is simply acting maturely, and shows the kind of honor and trustworthiness that is desirable in such a complex, demanding, long-term commitment as a marriage.

They may be terrified of questioning the other person for fear of exposing themselves, being rejected, and losing a potential partner. They hate being single. They feel frightened, frustrated, and lonely, and to them the pain of loneliness is more terrifying than making a bad choice. They are willing to make all kinds of promises and compromises just for the sake of having somebody to marry. Too often, once they're married, they forget the pain and discomfort of the single condition. Some things they closed their eyes to then come back to haunt them, and they refuse to live up to the commitments they have made. It is important to be honest about wanting to be married and to remember why you undertook the commitments you made. Fear of loneliness is not sufficient as the main reason to marry someone if there are no other reasons for choosing him or her. A marriage based on this motivation often does not endure.

You must remember that your happiness will be bound up with the person you marry. You'll have to share your children, the rewards and frustrations of work, and much time—day and night, weekends and holidays. You'll have to cope with his or her tastes if you don't share them. You'll have to help and sustain him or her through adversity and frustration. To choose someone only to escape loneliness through marriage only means you want to solve your own problems. You need a better reason for marriage than wanting to get out of a particular situation.

It has become fashionable to disregard background when selecting a spouse. It's very laudable and worthwhile to be fair and give everyone a chance on the basis of individual merit, and yet this accepting attitude is generally a mistaken approach to marriage. Being blind to reality does not help anyone, and since so much of personality is determined by background, it is very helpful in choosing a spouse—without prejudice or accusations, honestly and realistically—to explain your own background, to explore the other's background, and to deal openly with the information that emerges. By background I mean everything, or as much as possible of everything. This does not mean an account of every boring detail of your lives, but a careful examination of every background area. No area is sacred, no area should be taboo. Actually, if some area is considered taboo, it is particularly important to explore it to make sure that each partner will be able to handle it.

The factors that have an enormous influence on personality and thus on how you behave in marriage are: how many children there were in the family; what position you hold among the children; how old your parents were when you were born; what they did for a living; how well they got along; how long they lived, if they are dead; were they poor, were they rich; the life style in their home; their ethnic, religious, and political background; your own medical history including any psychiatric history; the way your parents treated you; the kind of house you grew up in; the cultural milieu you have known. If you're self-assured enough, you may say, "I'm marrying the person, not the family or background." I applaud that. But this brave approach to marriage, to be successful, must nonetheless be based on an understanding of the choice being made and its consequences, and the willingness and indeed the ability to live with those consequences. It shows that your love is strong if you marry someone knowing that something in his or her background means you are risking a possibly unfortunate outcome. It shows less love if you only know his or her evident strengths and abilities and have chosen to remain ignorant of some possibly unhappy implications of background facts you haven't even tried to discover. To learn enough to be able to say, if necessary, "I marry you in spite of this"—is surely a sign of love. At the same time, you should be willing to share with him or her information about your own background of which you may be ashamed or afraid—not in an attempt to threaten, tease, or drive the partner away, but as proof that you understand the seriousness of the undertaking, and that you want to make it as successful as possible.

When there is no attempt to select, people are treated as if they were of no importance, as though the situation of marriage were important but the partners in it are easily interchangable. Partners who become involved on this level are not prepared to deal with one another later as real people. They are not equipped to handle one another's weaknesses. They are not on the lookout for potential difficulties arising from each partner's individual and unique personality. As a physician, I think in terms of medical models. The best kind of medicine, the most effective and successful, is preventive medicine. The same applies to marriage. The best kind of marital therapy is the preventive therapy that takes place before marriage in careful self-examination and selection of a spouse.

The objective of the process is to select the most desirable spouse. Some human beings are more attractive, more intelligent, and more successful than others. Since you are looking for a potential mate "till death do us part," search for as emotionally and physically healthy, intelligent, and successful a human being as you can find. After the commitment is made, all your efforts should be directed toward maintaining it, but there is a time to evaluate, to bargain, to consider and reconsider, and that time is before the commitment has been made—most certainly before the legal commitment, the actual marriage ceremony, but ideally even before a firm emotional commitment, before the chosen person and his or her availability becomes enormously important to your happiness.

Fortunately, careful selection does not exclude anyone from the possibility of marrying. Actually, the careful selection of a spouse is an inclusive process. It leads people away from stereotypes about who makes a good spouse, and encourages them to make individualistic choices–choices that are right for them and not necessarily right for anybody else.

One extremely important background area is the parents' marriage. Much of what people observe as children becomes incorporated into their personalities, into their innermost being; and so, unfair as it may seem, people who have been so lucky as to be the products of happy marriages are themselves much better candidates for happy marriage than people who are the product of unhappy marriages. It *is* unfair, but that's how it is.

Does that mean that people who were children of unhappy marriages or divorced unions should be avoided as marital partners? Most certainly not. If you are the child of a troubled marriage, it does increase the chances of trouble in your own marriage, but if you are aware of this, and understand you are at risk, your chances of being able to do something about it increase. We all carry within us models of how to cope with life based on our early environment; the children of unhappy marriages have poor models as far as marriage is concerned. They are hampered by lack of knowledge about how to cope with the inevitable stresses of marriage–how to quarrel and make up, how to handle illness and other misfortunes. Also, they are likely to have been damaged by strife between their parents, so that their adult abilities to be empathetic, warm, sympathetic, and loving have been diminished. Since we all tend to use ourselves and our experiences as a norm, such people may not even know that they are sometimes cruel, failing to show love and warmth. When the person they are married to asks for affection or compassion, they are likely not to hear their requests, since their similar needs as children often went unheeded by their parents.

Other people who come from unhappy marriages are intensely, painfully aware of the misery they cause, and are full of good intentions. But they frequently skip over real difficulties and overidealize the marriage situation. They fantasize about themselves as ideal spouses and seek another ideal spouse and an ideal marriage. They do this because they do not have functional—realistic, and appropriate—internalized models of what is possible, and so have nothing to guide them but their own imagination, their own fantasy of what marriage should be. They are at times so totally unrealistic that even a good marriage probably disappoints them.

Therefore, be aware that if you are from a miserable or a broken home or are about to marry somebody who comes from one, you face a disadvantage. Such people are at risk, their marriages are at risk, and they have to try harder. In particular, you will need to be careful to recognize that whoever has this kind of unhappy background is likely to have faulty judgement about relationships, and therefore his or her opinions on relationships, including yours, cannot be taken uncritically, but must be carefully evaluated. This situation is of course still more complex and difficult if both partners have an unhappy childhood background.

There is no set of circumstances that guarantees that a marriage will be a hundred percent success. There are no specifics as to what the age of the partners should be, what the age differences should be, whether the male or the female should be older, who should be taller, better educated, smarter, richer, what their racial background should be, what their religious background should be. Nor is there a set of factors—illnesses, physical handicaps, religious barriers, educational barriers, racial barriers—that absolutely contraindicate marriage. The uniqueness of human beings makes any such specifics impossible. There are, however, some circumstances that help. There should be love in the marriage, and the potential spouse should be a loved person. People should seek marital partners whom they find sexually attractive. Try to find that kind of attraction right at the very beginning in your selection of a spouse.

Physically handicapped people can find marital partners. If they are psychologically sound and understand themselves and their situation, they can make excellent marriages. Marriages of people who have physical handicaps, if based on honest appraisal, acknowledgment, and acceptance of the handicap, have the real problem of adjusting to the world in terms of the handicap, but do not necessarily have to suffer any sexual or other dissatisfaction. Acknowledge that the physical aspect of marriage is important and accept only those limitations in your partner that do not matter to you. It does not matter at all whether they are important to your friends, your neighbors, your mother and father, your uncle or your aunt. They won't have to live with your spouse. You will have to live with him or her. Do not take somebody whose physical attributes are unacceptable to you. But once you have made sure that he or she is acceptable to you, forget about what other people think of him or her. A good sex life has many components, and being physically attractive is only one. There are very many other strong sensual elements. Do you express tenderness similarly? Do you agree in your sexual preferences? Do you live in such harmony that when the time comes for tenderness, you are open to it? If the answer to these questions is yes, you are likely to be highly desirable to each other.

Physical compatibility also plays a part in other activities. Physical prowess or limitations are important. For instance, a very physical person will want strenuous recreational activities; any great disparity in taste or abilities becomes something that both partners must be ready to handle.

In considering physical attributes, people should also consider the age difference. The greater the age difference between the partners, the greater the disparity or chance of disparity in their life spans and in their physical powers and agility. Age need not be a barrier to a happy marriage as long as the partners are aware of and can deal with the problems that any such disparity may bring. Successful marriages can have various combinations of ages; the combination chosen by the particular people just has to be satisfactory to them.

For reasons that are poorly understood, people are endowed with different degrees of vitality, and certain people live at a much faster tempo than others. If the partners are very different from each other in these respects they will have to learn to handle the difference. And even such a minor difference as being a "night person" or a "day person" can be important.

They will have to learn to cope with these differences in their temperaments.

Intellectual compatibility and equality help to build a harmonious marriage. Marriage is a relationship between peers; with the marriage there comes an equality between the partners. But if there are great differences in, for instance, age, former socioeconomic status, or educational background, the marital relationship is making equals of very differently endowed people. It has become increasingly necessary to be able to deal with life situations abstractly and to solve problems verbally. Marital partners need to do these things mutually, since their decisions should be based on a consensus, and it's extremely helpful if, in spite of any other differences between them, they think alike. If there is a great difference in intellectual capability, the smarter one will often have to listen to and go along with the ideas of the spouse, and does not have the right or prerogative to force his or her own will on the grounds of being smarter because, through marriage they have become peers with equal status.

Beyond this, it is helpful for the partners to be in general agreement about life, to have their priorities essentially in the same order, to have few important differences between them. The more the partners disagree, the more their priorities diverge, the greater their differences of all kinds, the more each must compromise to arrive at a mutually satisfactory arrangement.

Whether the decision is to have children or not to have children, the issue of parenthood is one about which each couple must make a joint decision. Most people already have some idea before getting married whether becoming parents is something they are for, against, or neutral about. Parents' physical, psychological, and intellectual characteristics are very apt to be handed down to children, through genetic inheritance and also by the psychological influence of the home environment. Also, we tend to raise our children the same way we were raised. Therefore, each spouse's childhood environment will have great influence on their own children, and this fact cannot be wished away and should be confronted.

It's extremely important to explore the issue of money before marriage, not only the concrete issue of how much money, but also the meaning of money to each partner. It seems to be much easier for people to talk to me about their sexual habits and preferences than about how much money they make or how much money they have. Money and its handling has enormous symbolic importance to people and is very much a part of the picture they have of themselves, particularly their idea of their self-worth or lack of it. Money's symbolic value is over and above its purchasing power, which is in itself important. The symbolic value intensifies the necessary real involvement with money. For the partners to have very different attitudes about money—how much they desire, why they desire it, and so on—can lead to very serious difficulties. For instance, if a person to whom money means success, power, beauty, and sex appeal marries one to whom money is not all that important, they are likely to have many differences of opinion about how to spend their time or invest their energies. One may want to work for money all the time, the other to take life easy. Such differences are likely to lead to emotion-laden arguments. Or if someone who feels that living on an inherited income is somehow dishonorable marries a spouse with a large inheritance, the issue of where this couple's own money should come from is likely to be a difficult source of trouble.

In exploring the ability to spend time together and get along with one another, the following questions may be helpful: "How pleasantly do we pass time together?" "How well do we communicate?" This means, "How freely, how openly, how smoothly do we talk to one another and how skillfully do we listen to one another? Do I listen, or while my friend is talking, perhaps saying something very personal, am I superimposing my own thoughts and ideas onto what is being said because I am afraid to hear what my friend is saying?" Often people are afraid to hear what the other person is saying, because then they will no longer be able to maintain fantasies about the other person unhampered by reality. No longer will they be able to attribute qualities to that person that he or she does not possess and that they desperately desire in a potential partner; consequently, that person will no longer be a marriage prospect. Here the fear of the loneliness of being single may be taking over. Ask, "Is the partnership a good combination? Is it likely to stand the test of time?" These are the issues that need to be explored and, once again, the best way to do it is to spend time together, talking and listening honestly to one another.

Should such careful selection of a spouse—spending much time together, exploring personalities, talking, questioning, observing reactions under diversified circumstances—include a trial marriage? After all, it might be easier to find out about each other by trying marriage, rather than by conversation, observation, introspection, and deduction.

I would like to be able to advocate trial marriage. I think a trial marriage would be a terrific rehearsal if it could be arranged. Unfortunately, it is not possible to have a trial marriage. You may have a friendship, a relationship, an arrangement, an affair, but you cannot have a trial marriage, because as long as it is a trial, it's not a marriage. One of the things that defines a marriage is that special security that comes from its permanence. Once you embark on marriage, you're on a permanent voyage. You have a bond that includes the commitment "till death do us part."

Premarital Sex. What about premarital sex, then? Will having it be helpful for marriage? And is it a good indicator of how successful marital sex with someone will be?

As everybody knows, there's a lot of extramarital sexual activity. However, only a very small percentage of extramarital sex is truly premarital sex—that is, sex undertaken specifically by two people to evaluate one another as possible marriage partners or sex with someone you're beginning to think of marrying. Sometimes people lie about a relationship, as one that could potentially lead to marriage, to win sexual favors. That, of course, is no kind of exploration in preparation for marriage, but an inducement to cajole someone into having sex. But is genuine premarital sex helpful in selecting a mate?

Premarital sex is not absolutely and definitely either beneficial or destructive to marriage itself, because the psychological factors in human sex determine how the sexual activity is experienced. There can be no simple rules about premarital sex. Statements such as, "Don't marry as a virgin because your inexperience will hurt your marriage"; or, "Be a virgin when you marry because your purity will guarantee your sexual happiness," simply are not valid. The best general suggestion I can make is, try to embark on your marriage in as good shape sexually—that is, as sexually aware, responsive, and able—as you possibly can.

What this advice means will vary from person to person. "Good shape" is not a matter of being sexually experienced or inexperienced. Depending on age, cultural milieu, social background, general life patterns, family, and other circumstances, it is good for some people to enter marriage with sexual experience, and for others it is good to enter marriage without it. Take someone who was given little correct information about sex when young and indeed grew up with a lot of misinformation. If he or she is fortunate enough to have sex before marriage in a romantic, private, comfortable place with an honorable and appealing person of the oppsoite sex, it may, even if it's not part of an intense on-going relationship, allow him or her to enter marriage relaxed, confident, optimistic, and cheerful about sex. On the other hand, for someone from a background where sex outside marriage was strictly forbidden, sexual experiences before marriage may be so burdened with tension and guilt that they will be harmful. Even if he or she experiments with sex to try to get rid of guilt about it, the guilt will hang on, especially if the partner does not indicate or have any interest in developing an emotional involvement, and rejects the guilty one's love. In sex, as in all other human endeavors, success breeds optimism and good feelings about self. Therefore it is wise to try to have sexual adventures that can be experienced as successful and enriching.

Premarital sex between a couple is not a good indicator of how successful their marital sex will be. Sex in marriage is a recurrent experience that the same partners share for a long time under very diversified circumstances. The long-term commitment and the fact that their sex life occurs while the partners are also dealing with many other problems of life make marital sex different. It is natural to desire and expect a satisfying sex life in marriage and, to that end, physical attraction and appeal between the partners are very important, but their presence is usually obvious to the partners before intercourse. If the attraction and appeal are present, usually intercourse will be fine, even great, both before and during the marriage. Of course it's good to know that your partner is sexually capable and sexually potent, and it's possible that through premarital sex you might discover some serious sexual problems in your partner. But any such problems will become apparent anyway during an honest courtship during which the couple are open with one another and talk about their difficulties. It's possible but most unlikely that someone with no sexual experience may have a sexual difficulty that he or she isn't aware of. Even virgins, from what they have heard, from adolescent self-stimulation, or their sensual reactions to the opposite sex, usually have an accurate sense of what their reactions will be, including possible difficulties. And if there is a serious sexual problem that will become manifest later on, there will also be related difficulties that honest talk will bring to the fore. Thus, as always in things to do with marriage, paying attention to the relationship will help show what it is and where it is headed.

Studies of human sexuality have proved without a doubt that only a very small number of cases of impotence and frigidity and other serious sexual problems are due to organic causes, and are therefore absolute and irreversible, barring a medical cure. The vast majority of cases of sexual dysfunction are due to psychological factors. And—the nub of the issue—only a few of these factors are due to traumatic and damaging childhood experiences. Much more commonly, cases of sexual dysfunction are episodic reflections of psychologically stressful events in an individual's present life. Therefore successful premarital sex is not a guarantee that marital sex will be successful no matter what happens to the couple. As helpful as it may seem to find one's potential spouse both physically attractive and physiologically capable during marriage, many factors will greatly influence the success of the sex act, central among which are the psychological factors influencing each of the partners.

Even physical attraction cannot be measured in absolute terms. One or a few isolated sexual experiences cannot indicate whether it will last in a marriage, because the qualities that make a person appealing to another person over a long time include those that express the internal person, which are very much influenced by psychological factors.

But none of this is meant to suggest that premarital sex with someone you later marry is necessarily harmful. Indeed, it may be useful if it reassures an individual about his or her sexuality or dispells some erroneous notions about sexuality. Under some circumstances it may be an esteem-building experience, teaching a person that he or she is desirable, potent, able to perform sexually, and able to enjoy sexuality. Or it may be useful in making a person feel more alive, more vigorous, more sensual. In essence, it may in one or more of these ways make a person feel more like a "special" person. For this to occur, the premarital sexual experience must be good, a "special" experience, and thus the opposite of most promiscuous sex. It should take place in a special setting under special circumstances to make people feel special. Unpremeditated, casual, haphazard, and unevaluated sex—that is, promiscuous sex—tends to erode feelings of specialness, as well as integrity and reliability. And, by and large, anything that diminishes these feelings also diminishes a person's feelings of security, and so is detrimental to well-being.

Usually people tend to get better at something they do a lot. Unfortunately, being sexually experienced with many people under many circumstances does not necessarily add to sexual prowess or make anyone a better lover. Nor is a random sampling of many sexual partners a good way to look for one who will make a sexually satisfying marital partner. I wish it could be that simple, but sexuality itself is so complicated that it does not lend itself to simple solutions. It's not a game of numbers in which, if only you try enough people, you'll find out what turns you on the most. On the contrary, promiscuous sex tends to be a somewhat barren sexual experience, and is sexually debilitating to most people.

Improving yourself sexually—making yourself a more sexually aware, responsive, and able person—is a complicated, multifaceted effort, and much of it has to take place intrapsychically. No amount of experimentation can guarantee a good sex life because, although sex is a physical activity, it is experienced intrapsychically. Thus only an understanding of the psychology involved can change it, make it better. Just having sex—just doing sex, as it were—does not help. What does help is trying to understand yourself as a sexual person—your priorities, pace, values—and to find a mode of sexual expression that is in harmony with who you are. A good sex life is psychologically a very subtle and sensitive matter. If you merely insist on physical expression and let things go at that, you belittle both sex and yourself.

CHAPTER 8

In Defense of Marriage

Some of the steps most necessary for a good marriage have taken place in the childhood years when the personality is formed. Some environments produce better candidates for marriage than others. Of course, you didn't and couldn't choose your parents, or the time or place of your birth. However, one important step you can take to prepare yourself for a good marriage is to evaluate yourself and achieve some measure of self-knowledge. You must ask yourself, "Is marriage what I want? Is it right for me? Is it the life style within which my goals and hopes are most likely to be fulfilled?"

Consider also very carefully whether you really want what marriage offers—its disadvantages, restrictions, and limitations as well as its advantages, among which is its promise of love. Married love is binding, demanding, and exclusive, and as such it is not always easy to sustain. However, it is the basic strength of a good marriage, its magic, its cement, its very backbone. Anything that detracts from this love detracts from the security and appeal of marriage. Ask yourself, "Am I ready right now to embark on marriage? Am I ready for an exclusive love relationship? Are permanence and loyalty and support at time of need worth their price of commitment from me, a commitment to love and support in return? Am I ready to deal with the fact that this love and security demands exclusiveness, and bars me from other relationships, from other styles of living?"

If you can answer with "yes," you're basically ready for marriage. If you can't say "yes," without reservations or doubts, you may get married, but you'll have difficulty. Some measure of ambivalence in this matter is normal and inevitable, but at least on the conscious level you should feel a deliberate desire to make the commitment, even if you think you're not quite ready, and even if you're aware it will not be easy.

You must also understand that marriage implies an exclusive monogamous sexual relationship—heterosexual, by definition—and thus demands that you enter into no other sexual relationships. Any extramarital sex is a mistake, and will require forgiveness and working through by both partners, or at least concealment from the other. It is never helpful. It is true that many marriages go on in spite of numerous and repeated affairs, but that merely goes to prove that, as an institution, marriage can survive under the worst of circumstances. At the least you must understand that you're promising to close off other sexual relationships; if you're fascinated by a diversity of sexual partners, then marriage is not for you at the moment.

Certainly one of the genuine advantages of marriage is that it provides a companion, a mate, a friend, someone whose interests—self-interests, that is—are the same as your own. If you do not feel the need to alleviate loneliness, you are not a good candidate for marriage. If you perceive marital companionship as stifling and confining, you are not a good candiate for marriage. You must be willing, even if you are ambivalent about it, to spend time with your spouse on good days as well as bad. A married person must be at least willing and ideally will look forward to mutuality and sharing of time, hopes, aspirations, problems, wishes, and desires—not just one partner's but both. If you do not see marriage as a two-way street, and if you aren't willing to share, your marriage will rest on very shaky foundations.

Sharing includes all the areas expressed in the marriage service: for better or for worse, for richer or poorer, through sickness and health, forsaking all others. Your partner promises that and so do you. It is that commitment that makes marriage what it is—a long-term arrangement, not immediate gratification at all times under all circumstances. Long-term goals require maturity, internal strength, and internal health. A mature person is not someone who cannot enjoy, who cannot play, who postpones pleasure indefinitely. A mature person also is not someone who always plays, looks for gratification and pleasure everywhere, and demands immediate expression of instinctual drives. A mature person is someone who realistically reconciles the various aspects of personality and life, and who finds fulfillment in the supportive institution of marriage. For such a person marriage is the best framework for life, and a wonderful help in achieving all long-term goals—work, raising children, building a career, gaining financial security. There is no other institution with the advantages or degree of companionship it brings.

For some individuals, however, marriage is wrong. They are not suited for marriage, just as others are not suited to be astronauts, politicians, actors, or surgeons. If such a person marries, there will be problems for him or her, but those problems are not the fault of the institution, and marriage as a way of life is not to blame for them. Some people choose to marry the wrong partners; they are inevitably going to have trouble, but again it's not the fault of the institution. The problems are caused by the fact that the people involved are unsuited to one another.

Every marriage has two particular people in it who need to work life out in their own way. They must adjust to each other, to their children, to what society wants, to whatever changes occur in their relationship.

The reason marriage endures as an institution is that it satisfies basic psychological needs. The quality of human life depends on the quality of the relationships of the person who is living that life. Relationships with other people are what make a life good, tolerable, excellent, or dismal. Whether you perceive your life as successful or miserable is very much a measure of how you perceive your relationships with other people. That is why people in similar circumstances can be happy or unhappy. That's why the rich or the famous are not immune to misery, and why ordinary people are able to find a great deal of happiness.

People seek psychiatric help for many problems but very often what finally drives people into treatment is a deterioration of their relationships with others. Consequently, one good measure of treatment's success is an improvement in relationships.

The central relationship of any adult life is with one's mate; in my opinion, marriage, conventional, permanent, monogamous marriage, is the ideal way to achieve happiness in that relationship. I'm not saying that miserable and unhappy marriages don't exist, or marriages with problems, or that being married solves all human problems, What I am saying is that marriage always implies three things—permanence, sexual exclusiveness, and dedication. Some circumstances reflect good fortune. Other circumstances reflect personal choice and are therefore negotiable; but these three basic aspects generate security and mutual trust in the partners, and liberate them to grow and develop. When this does not happen, it isn't the problem of the institution, but of the partners.

No other form of cohabitation can compete with marriage. It has maintained itself through centuries of political, economic and technical upheaval. A marriage can make people happy whether they have children or not, whether the man supports the family, or the woman works, or whether both do. It doesn't matter what their priorities are as far as success, how they spend their money, what they do for recreation, how much companionship they need, how they like to have sex—all these are merely preferences, all negotiable and subject to individual choices. Married people may evolve very personalized life styles, but again, the permanence, the sexual exclusiveness, the dedication to each other are not negotiable. They are the absolute foundation of marriage, and anything that damages them cracks the foundation on which every marriage is based.

References

1. *Therapy for Couples.* Billie S. Ables in collaboration with Jeffrey N. Brandsma. (Washington, D.C.: Jossey-Bass, 1977).

2. *Treating the Troubled Family.* Nathan W. Ackerman (New York: Basic Books, 1966).

3. *Parenthood - Its Psychology and Psychopathology.* E. James Anthony, Therese Benedek ed. (Boston: Little, Brown and Company, 1970).

4. *Handbook of Marriage Counseling.* Ben N. Ard, Jr., Constance C. Ard, eds. (Palo Alto, Calif.: Science and Behavior Books, 1969).

5. *American Handbook of Psychiatry,* 2nd Edition. *Silvano Arieti,* ed. (New York: Basic Books, 1974).

6. *Love Can Be Found.* Silvano Arieti, James Arieti. (New York: Harcourt Brace Jovanovich, 1977).

7. *Helping Parents Help Their Children.* L. Eugene Arnold ed. (New York: Brunner Mazel, 1978).

8. *Basic Child Psychiatry.* Philip Barker. (New York: Science House, 1971).

9. *Homosexualities—A Study of Diversity Among Men and Women,* an Official Publication of the Institute for Sex Research founded by Alfred C. Kinsey, Alan P. Bell, Martin S. Weinberg. (Simon & Schuster, 1978).

10. *Money and Emotional Conflicts—The Unconscious Roots of Money Neurosis.* Edmund Bergler. (New York: International Universities Press, 1959).

11. *The Children of the Dream.* Bruno Bettelheim. (New York: Macmillan Company, 1969).

12. *Attachment and Loss,* volumes I and II. John Bowlby. (New York: Basic Books, 1969).

13. *The Sex Researchers.* Edward M. Brecher. (Boston: Little, Brown & Co., 1969).

14. *Mothers, Fathers and Children.* Sylvia Brody and Sidney Axelrad. (New York: International Universities Press, 1978).

15. *Two Worlds of Childhood, U.S. and U.S.S.R.* Urie Bronfenbrenner. (New York: Russell Sage Foundation, 1970).

16. *Troubled Children in a Troubled World.* Edith Buxbaum. (New York: International Universities Press, 1970).

17. *Handbook of Marriage and the Family.* Harold T. Christensen ed. (Chicago: Rand McNally & Company, 1964).

18. *The Joy of Sex.* Alex Comfort. (Simon & Schuster, 1972).

19. *Sexual Attraction.* Mark Cook, Robert McHenry. (New York: Pergamon Press, 1978).

20. *Human Autoerotic Practices.* Manfred F. DeMartino. (New York: Human Sciences Press, 1979).

21. *Divorced in America.* Joseph Epstein. (New York: E. P. Dutton and Co., 1974).

22. *Childhood and Society.* Erik H. Erikson. (New York: W.W. Norton & Company, 1950).

23. *Identity - Youth and Crisis.* Erik H. Erikson. (New York: W.W. Norton & Company, 1968).

24. *Phenomenology and Treatment of Anxiety.* William E. Fann, Ismet Karacan, Alex D. Pokorny, Robert L. Williams, eds. (New York: Spectrum Publications, 1979).

25. *Adolescent Psychiatry. Volume IV.* Sherman C. Feinstein, Peter Giovacchini eds. (New York: Jason Aronson, 1975).

26. *Adolescent Psychiatry. Volume V.* Sherman C. Feinstein, Peter Giovacchini, eds. (New York: Jason Aronson, 1975).

27. *Conjoint Marital Therapy.* R. V. Fitzgerald. (New York: Jason Aronson, 1973).

28. *Comprehensive Textbook of Psychiatry,* 3rd edition. *Alfred M. Freedman,* Harold I. Kaplan, Benjamin J. Sadock, eds. (Baltimore: Williams and Wilkins, 1975).

29. *The Writings of Anna Freud. Volume 3. Infants without Families* (New York: International Universities Press, 1973).

30. *Sigmund Freud, Collected Papers,* Volume I. Authorized translation under the supervision of Joan Riviere. (New York: Basic Books, 1959).

31. *Sigmund Freud, Collected Papers.* Volume V. James Strachey, ed. (New York: Basic Books, 1959).

32. The *Sexual Enlightenment of Children.* Sigmund Freud. (New York: Collier Books, 1966).

33. *Sexuality and the Psychology of Love.* Sigmund Freud. (New York: Collier Books, 1966).

34. *Psychotherapy wiith Children of Divorce.* Richard A. Gardner. (New York: Jason Aronson, 1976).

35. *Understanding Children.* Richard A. Gardner. (New York: Jason Aronson, 1973).

36. *Sexual Suicide.* George F. Gilder. (New York: Quadrangle The New York Times Book Co., 1973).

37. *Human Sexuality.* Richard Green, ed. (Baltimore: Williams and Wilkins Co., 1979).

38. *Assessment of Sexual Function.* Group for the Advancement of Psychiatry. (New York: Jason Aronson, 1974).

39. *Couples in Conflict.* Alan S. Gurman, David G. Rice. (New York: Jason Aronson, 1975).

40. *The Sex Atlas.* Erwin J. Haeberle. (New York: A Continuum Book, The Seabury Press, 1978).

41. *Changing Families.* Jay Haley. (New York: Grune and Stratton, 1971).

42. *Learning to Love.* Harry F. Harlow. (New York: Jason Aronson, 1974).

43. *The Anatomy of Loneliness* Joseph Hartog, J. Ralph Audy, and Yehudi A. Cohen, eds. (New York: International Universities Press, 1980).

44. *Changing Homosexuality in the Male.* Lawrence J. Hatterer. (New York: McGraw-Hill Co., 1970).

45. *A Textbook of Psychiatry. Sir David Henderson*, R. D. Gillespie, Ivor R. C. Batchelor. (New York: Oxford University Press, 1956).

46. *The Hite Report.* Shere Hite. (New York: MacMillan Publishing Co., and London: Collier MacMillan, 1976).

47. *Human Emotions.* Carroll E. Izard. (New York: Plenum Press, 1977).

48. *The Psychology of Adolescence.* Arthur T. Jersild, Judith S. Brook, David W. Brook. (New York: Macmillan Publishing Co., 1978).

49. *Birth to Maturity.* Jerome Kagan, Howard A. Moss. (New York: John Wiley, and Sons, 1962).

50. *Child Psychiatry.* Leo Kanner. (Springfield, Ill.: Charles C. Thomas, 1957).

51. *The Illustrated Manual of Sex Therapy.* Helen Singer Kaplan. (Quadrangle, New York Times Book Co., 1975).

52. *The New Sex Therapy.* Helen Singer Kaplan. (New York: Brunner Mazel, 1974).

53. *Internal World and External Reality.* Otto F. Kernberg, M.D. (New York; Jason Aronson, 1980).

54. *The Universal Experience of Adolescence.* Norman Kiell (New York: International Universities Press, 1964).

55. *The Sexual Behavior in the Human Male.* Alfred C. Kinsey, Wardell B. Pomeroy, Clyde E. Martin. (Philadelphia: W. B. Saunders Co., 1948).

56. *Woman's Orgasm.* Georgia Kline-Graber and Benjamin Graber. (New York: Bobbs-Merrill Co., 1975).

57. *The Analysis of the Self.* Heinz Kohut. (New York: International Universities Press, 1971).

58. *The Sexually Responsive Woman.* Phyllis and Eberhard Kronhausen. (New York: The Grove Press, Inc., 1964).

59. *Schizophrenia and the Family.* Theodore Lidz, Stephen Fleck, Alice R. Cornelison. (New York: International Universities Press, 1965).

60. *Medical Aspects of Human Sexuality.* Harold I. Lief. ed. (Baltimore: Williams & Wilkins Co., 1975).

61. *Perversions, Psychodynamics and Therapy.* Sandor Lorand, Michael Balint, eds. (New York: Random House, 1956).

62. *The Father—His Role in Child Development.* David B. Lynn. (Monterey, Calif.: Brooks/Cole Publishing Co., a Division of Wadsworth Publishing Co., 1974).

63. *Treatment For Children.* David Maclay. (New York: Science House, 1970).

64. *Masturbation From Infancy to Senescence.* Irwin M. Marcus, John J. Francis. eds. (New York: International Universities Press, 1975)

65. *Human Sexual Inadequacy.* William H. Masters, Virginia E. Johnson (Boston: Little, Brown & Co., 1970).

66. *Human Sexual Response.* William H. Masters, Virginia E. Johnson. (Boston: Little, Brown & Co., 1966).

67. *Incest.* Karin C. Meiselman. (Washington, D.C.: Jossey-Bass, 1978).

68. *Exploring Intimate Life Styles.* Bernard I. Murstein, ed. (New York: Springer Publishing Co., 1978).

69. *Open Marriage.* Nena O'Neill, George O'Neill. (New York: M. Evans and Co., 1972).

70. *The Harvard Guide to Modern Psychiatry.* Armand M. Nicholi, Jr., ed. (Cambridge, Mass.: Belknap Press of Harvard University Press, 1978).

71. *Basic Handbook of Child Psychiatry.* Joseph D. Noshpitz, ed. (New York: Basic Books, 1979).

72. *The Joy of Suffering.* Shirley Panken. (New York: Jason Aronson, 1973).

73. *The Theory and Practice of Psychiatry.* Fredrick C. Redlich, Daniel X. Freedman. (New York: Basic Books, 1966).

74. *Dual-Career Marriage.* David G. Rice. (New York: The Free Press, a division of Macmillan Publishing Co., 1979).

75. *Perspectives in Child Psychopathology.* Herbert E. Rie, ed. (New York: Aldine Atherton, 1971).

76. *The Sexual Experience.* Benjamin J. Sadock, Harold I. Kaplan, Alfred M. Freedman, eds. (Baltimore: Williams and Wilkins Co., 1976).

77. *Latency.* Charles Sarnoff. (New York: Jason Aronson, 1976).

78. *Mayer-Gross Slater, Roth, eds. Clinical Psvchiatry.* 3rd edition. Eliot Slater, Martin Roth, eds.(London: Baillière Tindall, 1977).

79. *Beyond Monogamy.* James R. Smith, Lynn G. Smith. eds. (Baltimore: The Johns Hopkins University Press, 1974).

80. *Homosexuality.* Charles W. Socarides. (New York: Jason Aronson, 1978).

81. *Children of the Kibbutz.* Melford E. Spiro. (New York: Schocken Books, 1968).

82. *The First Year of Life.* René A. Spitz. (New York: International Universities Press, 1965).

83. *Klemer's Counseling in Marital and Sexual Problems.* Robert F. Stahmann, William J. Hiebert, eds. (Baltimore: Williams & Wilkins Co., 1977).

84. *Sexual Excitement.* Robert J. Stoller. (New York: Pantheon Books, 1979).

85. *The Competent Infant* L. Joseph Stone, Henrietta T. Smith, Lois B. Murphy. (New York: Basic Books, 1973).

86. *The Extramarital Affair.* Herbert S. Strean. (New York: The Free Press, A Division of Macmillan Publishing Co., 1980).

87. *Love and Limerance.* Dorothy Tennov. (New York: Stein & Day, 1979).

88. *Children of Parting Parents.* Lora Heims Tessman. (New York: Jason Aronson, 1978).

89. *Temperament and Behavior Disorders in Children.* Alexander Thomas, Stella Chess, Herbert G. Birch. (New York: New York University Press, 1968).

90. *Sex Research.* Martin S. Weinberg, ed. (New York: Oxford University Press, 1976).

91. *Children Under Stress.* Sula Wolff. (London: Allen Lane, The Penguin Press, 1969).

Index

Abortion, 90
Adoption, 109, 111-112
Adversity, support in, 157
Age differences in marriage, 178
Alcohol
  effects on marriage, 78-79
  effects on sexual activity, 78
Amniocentesis, 96, 106
Anal sex, 76
Aphrodisiacs, 66, 67
Artificial insemination, 109, 111
Avoidance of sex, 55

Bigamous relationships, 15
Bisexuality, 18, 58

Capacity for intimacy, 161
Children
  considerations about number to have, 102-105
  considerations as to why and when to have them, 94, 102, 179
  discovery by them of parents in intercourse, 65
  handicapped, 113
  in marriage, 89
Communes, 18, 20
Companionship, 150
  and clinging, 152-153
  dependency needs, 162
Contraception, 89
  condoms, 90
  diaphragms, 90
  pill, 89
  rhythm method, 90
  sterilization, 90
  vasectomy, 90

Dependency needs, 152-153, 162
Differences in sexual appetites, 44-55
Drugs, 81
  effects on marriage, 82
  effects on sex, 82

Egocentricity, 166
Extralegal alternatives, 20
Extramarital affairs, 42-52, 188

Foreplay, 48, 69
  stressful, 70-71
Frigidity, 55

Group sexual relationships, 15, 18

Handicapped children, 113
  partners, 178
Home, 138-142
Homosexuality, 15, 18, 50
  latent, 75

Illness, 84
  as relating to sexual performance, 84
Impotence, 55
Infertility, 110
Internal reality versus external reality, 24
Intercourse
  discontent after, 75
  mechanics of, 73-75
  reaction of children to, 65
  variations, 72

Love
  and possessiveness, 148

in marriage, 145

Male and female roles in marriage, 128
Marriage
age differences between partners in, 178
alcoholism in, 78-79
and love, 145
children in, 89, 91
criticism of, 16
drugs in, 82
male and female roles in, 128
maturity regarding, 167
personality factors which influence, 174
physical handicaps in, 178
practical side of, 117
recreation in, 154
sex in, 37
strengths of, 19
stress in, 23
what it offers, 15
Mobility
role of it in need for forming temporary rather than permanent relationships, 17
Money, 129
and work, 132-136
as weapon, 136
meaning of, 180

Oral sex, 75
Oversensitivity, 164-166

Parenthood, whether to have children or not, 94-105, 179
Parent's marriage as influence on children's chances
of good relationship in marriage, 176
Physical handicaps in marriage, 177
Pornography as a turn-on, 82-83
Possessions, 142
Possessiveness, 148
Premarital sex, 181-185
Psychosexual illnesses, 55, 84

Rape, 55
Reaction to interruption of intercourse by children, 65
Recreation, 154-156
Roles
male and female, 128

Sadomasochism, 83-84
Secondary gain from illness, 30
Self stimulation, 41
Separation, 40
Sex
anal, 76-77
and alcohol, 78
and drugs, 82
as a weapon, 62
education, 87
manuals of, 85
oral, 75
to reinforce self-esteem, 61
varieties of marital, 63
Sexual
advantages in marriage, 37-40, 64
differences in appetite, 45-46
identity as realized through parental roles, 93
infidelity, 41
molestation, 55
nonexclusiveness, 14
one-night stands, 39
possible problems, 40-52
preference, 63
timing of activity, 66
Sibling relationships as prototypes for communal ones, 20
Spouse selection, 168-170
biological factors in, 172
conscious elements in, 171
effect of parent's marital happiness on potential spouse, 176
unconscious elements in, 168-170
Stress
contagiousness of, 32
dealing with, 32
in foreplay, 70-71
in marriage, 23
one partner's, 36
unresolved early, 24

Sublimation, 41
Substitute sexual partners, 41
Support in adversity, 157
Swinging, 18

Tolerance for frustration, 164

Unresolved early stress, 24

Work, 117-128
  and money, 132